D0939097

VEDANTA

VEDANTA

Heart of Hinduism

❦

HANS TORWESTEN

Adapted by
LOLY ROSSET
From a Translation from the German by
JOHN PHILLIPS

GROVE WEIDENFELD
New York

181.48
Tow

Copyright © 1985 by Walter-Verlag AG, Olten
Translation copyright © 1991 by Grove Press, Inc.

All rights reserved.

No part of this book may be reproduced, stored in a retrieval system,
or transmitted in any form, by any means, including mechanical, electronic,
photocopying, recording, or otherwise, without prior written permission of
the publisher.

Published by Grove Weidenfeld
A division of Grove Press, Inc.
841 Broadway
New York, NY 10003-4793

Published in Canada by General Publishing Company, Ltd.

Grateful acknowledgment is made to the Ramakrishna-Vivekananda Center
for permission to reprint excerpts from:
The Upanishads: volumes I–IV, by Swami Nikilananda (translator), as published by the
Ramakrishna-Vivekananda Center of New York, copyright 1949, 1952, 1956, and 1959, by
Swami Nikhilananda; and *The Bhagavad Gita,* by Swami Nikhilananda (translator), as
published by the Ramakrishna-Vivekananda Center of New York, copyright 1944, by Swami
Nikhilananda.

Library of Congress Cataloging-in-Publication Data

Torwesten, Hans, 1944–
[Vedanta, Kern des Hinduismus. English]
Vedanta, heart of Hinduism / by Hans Torwesten ; adapted by Loly
Rosset from a translation from the German
by John Phillips. — 1st ed.
p.   cm.
Translation of: Vedanta, Kern des Hinduismus.
Includes bibliographical references.
ISBN 0-8021-1042-8 (acid-free paper)
1. Vedanta.   I. Rosset, Loly.   II. Title.   III. Title: Vedanta.
B132.V3T6713   1991
181'.48—dc20
90-37901
CIP

Manufactured in the United States of America

Printed on acid-free paper

Designed by Irving Perkins Associates

First English-language Edition 1991

10   9   8   7   6   5   4   3   2   1

Contents

VEDANTA

Introduction

ALTHOUGH OFTEN REGARDED as the most representative form of Eastern mysticism and metaphysics, Vedanta has not achieved the same degree of popularity in the West as have yoga and Zen. This may well be because they are connected with certain practices and the average person is familiar with them—if only by name—through a flood of course offerings (in which yoga is often only identified with *hatha-yoga* exercises nowadays). Vedanta, by contrast, is looked upon more as some kind of abstruse metaphysics, something for the head and accessible only to an intellectual elite. On the other hand, there are numerous contemporary attempts at popularization that see Vedanta as the sum total of all religions and philosophical systems, a perennial philosophy in its simplest and most concentrated form, universal religion as such, which, once the tangled vines of excessive Eastern exotica are removed, would actually make sense to a child.

Both the overly complicated and the oversimplified approaches make access to Vedanta unnecessarily difficult, of course, because both encourage the misconception that Vedanta addresses itself exclusively to the intellect. Hence it seems to some more difficult than Kant, Hegel, and Schelling combined; to others it can be reduced to a few handy concepts—*Brahman, Atman, maya, reincarnation,* and the like—by which the world's riddle can be cracked open at once.

Of course, Vedanta does want to be understood and, like all other worldviews and religions, it does try to find out "what deep within it holds this universe together," to borrow a phrase from Goethe's *Faust.* Still, when all has been clarified, something inexpressible remains in true Vedanta, something revealing itself only in inner mystical awareness, retaining something mysterious even in revelation. Just like Taoism, Zen Buddhism, Sufism, and Christian mysticism, Vedanta is above all a *way* that must be *walked.* It aims at man's center, his deepest intuition, where the light of truth suddenly shines forth. Its emphasis is on experience and realization. Where this is no longer the case we have merely an empty facade before us, a system, an ideology, one among many others. Where Vedanta has retained its vitality, what the Benedictine father LeSaux (Swami Abhishiktananda)—who lived and died in India—has said about the Upanishads also holds true for all of Vedanta: "It cannot be emphasized enough that this experience [of Atman-Brahman reality] has its origin at the deepest level of our being. The call of the Upanishads comes from a realm which transcends space and time. Its voice springs from silence. It seeks to awaken man and lead him back to himself. Just like the guru, the sacred books too are the mirror in which man progressively discovers himself and eventually recognizes the innermost truth about himself.

The moment comes when the spark flies across from one pole to the other. After that there is nothing but clear light everywhere—and in it have vanished, the master, the disciple, and even the sacred scriptures. . . ."[1]

Historically, Vedanta grew on Indian soil and in many respects coincides with what is commonly called Hinduism—although the two terms cannot be used synonymously. On the one hand, Vedanta is representative of only *one* system within Hinduism; it is one of the six *darshanas* (lit., way of seeing, viewpoint) that the Hindu considers orthodox, as distinguished from the heterodox systems of Jainism and Buddhism. One should not, however, imagine the six systems to be held in equally high regard and to be playing an equally important role in the religious life of today's Hindu. Some of these schools are today only of interest to academic specialists, for instance the *Nyaya* (Logic), the *Vaisheshika* (Teaching of Individual Characteristics), or the *Karma Mimansa*, the school concerned with the ritual aspect of the Vedas. *Sankhya* and, above all, the yoga system of *Patanjali* are far more widely known than those schools; they even occasionally compete with Vedanta. However, since these schools have over time not only attacked but also cross-fertilized one another, the lines of demarcation have often become very fluid. Much of the cosmology and psychology of the Sankhya system and many of its yoga methods were absorbed into Vedanta. It soon proved to be the most receptive and universal of all these schools, so that Vedanta is identified by many today as Hindu philosophy as such, the basis underlying the innumerable groupings, and the keynote in the melodious symphony of the Indian subcontinent; although many would go even further. In their opinion this Vedantic foundation—which at the same time is a crowning superstructure—far exceeds the bounds of an indigenous Hinduism and is even capable of appealing to Westerners who do not necessarily care to become Hindus in the narrower sense of the word (and strictly speaking, cannot).

The teachings of Vedanta, especially as reflected in the Upanishads and the Bhagavad Gita, aroused the interest of Western scholars, philosophers, and literary figures as early as the eighteenth and nineteenth centuries. It is well known that Wilhelm von Humboldt thanked God for having permitted him to live long enough to become acquainted with the Gita. Equally famous is Schopenhauer's enthusiasm. He declared that he derived much solace from the Upanishads when it came to his own life and death. As early as 1808, Friedrich Schlegel, the intellectual leader of the Romantic school in Germany, wrote *On the Language and Wisdom of the Indians,* acting, as it were, on behalf of many Romantics whose nostalgia for the Catholic Middle Ages combined with a yearning for India. This enthusiasm was supported, especially in the Anglo-Saxon world, by a philological meticulousness which, little by little, brought India's spiritual treasures to light. In this connection names like Max Müller and Paul Deussen must be given special mention. After the advent of Kant, the impact of German Idealism, and the ruminations of Schopenhauer, Germany was particularly receptive to the teachings of Vedanta—which in the process had also, of course, often to suffer being viewed through the spectacles of one or the other of these German philosophers.

This is not the place to mention all the scholars and writers in Europe and America who found their spiritual home in the wisdom of the East, or proved to be at least inspired by this wisdom. All of this interest extended initially not much beyond a small group of individuals, but it happened to coincide with a wave of spiritual expansion in India that suddenly began to inundate the West. This new expansion manifested itself in what seem like its most essential features at the end of the nineteenth century in the figure of Swami Vivekananda, the great disciple of Ramakrishna. It was Ramakrishna who, on the occasion of the Parliament of Religions at the Chicago World's Fair in 1893, appeared like an Eastern comet in the Western spiritual sky and brought the word Vedanta into circulation. It seemed to him most aptly to reflect the heart of the Hindu view of religion. Hindus themselves referred to their religion as *sanatana dharma* (eternal religion). Vivekananda was facing the task of familiarizing Westerners with his master Ramakrishna's universal message and the quintessence of the sanatana dharma without the necessity on the part of Americans or Europeans to have to grapple with the many local deities and caste restrictions of popular Hinduism.

Of course, Vivekananda did not invent Vedanta. He only simplified and modernized the ancient teachings of the Upanishads concerning the innately divine nature of man and pointed to the various yogic paths leading to highest realization of the Self. He did not establish any new universal religion. Like his master Ramakrishna, he pointed out that all religious paths—when truly looked upon as *paths* and not as mutually exclusive institutions—together already constitute a great universal religion. He wanted above all to bring Vedantic wisdom out into the open, to wrench it from the hands of a few pundits and priests. This, of course, led him to be reproached with watering down Vedanta and making it "palatable." However justified such reproach may be when it comes to oversimplification and popularization in general, in the case of Vivekananda it misses the essential point; for here simplification means *intensification*. His discourses do not, after all, come from the lips of a scribe who enjoys grappling with finicky scholastic detail, nor from the lips of an oversimplifier who merely seeks to appeal to the pigeonhole thinking of the masses, but from the lips of a realized yogi, someone enlightened who, like all great mystics, is at all times really only concerned with the *One*. Meister Eckhart, too, was often reproached for having spread the profoundest mystical truths among the common folk in simple (and lively!) language; but anyone who reads the sermons of this master—who in so many ways resembles the combative Vivekananda—will be hard put to conclude that he watered down truth.

We thus arrive at the question of how those of us who are not academically trained Sanskrit scholars but only interested lay persons ought to approach Vedanta. Should we completely ignore the modern interpretations of neo-Vedanta, or neo-Hinduism, so-called, and only consult such "source material" as the Upanishads, the Bhagavad Gita, and the Brahma Sutras, adding to these perhaps some of the classical commentaries on these scriptures, such as those by Shankara, Ramanuja, and others? Or should we take up one of those "textbooks" on Vedanta, those very simplified versions that were produced in great numbers as early as the Middle Ages—a kind of school catechism where the "truths" of Vedanta philosophy are presented in a neat and tidy way—as for instance the Vedantasara?

Our approach depends, of course, to a large degree on the why of such study, and here the lines of demarcation are also often blurred. It is entirely possible for someone sincerely striving spiritually to get completely hung up on some learned detail now and then; while someone else, who originally set out merely to enlarge his knowledge by one more system, may suddenly discover that his pursuit of intellectual knowledge has merely obscured his thirst for a deeper level of understanding. A book such as this must take both into account. Within a limited framework I am particularly addressing the reader who is looking for a first overall survey of Vedantic thought, but who at the same time would like to be led right into the heart of this spiritual view of life. The intention is neither to offer derivative and oversimplified concepts, nor to cause the reader to stumble continually over a mass of abstruse so-called source material. The pleasure a Westerner takes in the study of the spiritual world of India can be spoiled as much by excessive attention to detail—an endless series of which leaves him in a state of general perplexity—as by excessive missionary zeal. Those who plunge without any preparation into the jungles of the Brihadaranyaka Upanishad or who see themselves confronted right at the beginning with the dry-as-sticks and difficult Brahma Sutras will probably forgo any further study of Vedanta.

It is therefore not necessarily a disadvantage if we first encounter Vedanta in its modern attire: in the words of Ramakrishna, in the discourses of Vivekananda, or in the sayings of Ramana Maharshi. To begin with, this will make us realize that we are not dealing with spiritual fossils, with philosophical and religious archaeology, but with a truth that is alive and the everlastingness of which requires that it periodically be given new expression. In certain respects these modern mystics have much more in common with the original seers of the Upanishads than with the systematizers of the Middle Ages. Much of the medieval attire has dropped away and something of the original joy of discovery, of the pioneering spirit, is in evidence again. Of course, this in no way holds true for all those "gurus" who have now made Vedanta into a slick, fashionable, and barely recognizable philosophy. But then again, the latter should not be allowed to obscure the light of those who have revealed to the modern Western world the living spirit of Vedanta.

Many will no doubt prefer initially to try the ancient scriptures, and here it is clearly important to select those that render the Vedanta teachings at their most lucid, most lively, and most inspiring. Among these are the shorter Upanishads—such as the Isha, Katha, and Mundaka Upanishads, for instance—as well as selected texts from the longer Brihadaranyaka and Chandogya Upanishads, both belonging to the so-called older Upanishads. Then there is, of course, the Bhagavad Gita and, as an introduction to classical Advaita Vedanta, some of the shorter texts by Shankara such as the Atmabodha and the Viveka-cudamani. From this sound basis anyone can feel his way onward according to inclination; some, for instance, may want to acquaint themselves with the mythological strata we still find evidence of in the ancient world of the Upanishads; or plough through all the commentaries, the attempts to elucidate the brief cryptic aphorisms of the Brahma Sutras. Portions of these commentaries are rather dated, for instance the often lengthy polemical debates with the various Buddhist schools and the dualistic Sankhya system. These debates often remind us of the bitter disputes among various schools during our Western Middle Ages about how many angels could dance on the head of a pin. And just as it was important in the West, then, to break through this crust of so-called learnedness time and again to the spirit of Christ, so too in India forging ahead time and again to reach the living breath and spirit of Vedanta and allow oneself to be moved by it became an important task.

Nomen est omen. The word Vedanta itself points to its essential nature. Outwardly, *Veda-anta* only means "end of the Vedas," a purely factual reference to the final scriptures in the Vedic literature, namely the Upanishads. But just as in the eyes of the Christian the New Testament does not merely outwardly conclude the literature of the Bible but also inwardly "fulfills" and transcends all that preceded it, so here too *anta* means not only "end" but also "culmination" and "going beyond"—not only with respect to the Vedic scriptures but with respect to all that we are capable of knowing. For *veda* means knowledge, and Vedanta is thus what transcends all (relative) knowledge. "What is that by knowing of which all is known?" runs the famous and crucial question in the Mundaka Upanishad. (I.i.3) The answer is that there are two kinds of knowledge, the "lower" and the "higher." Among the lower are included the study of the Vedic texts: The Rig Veda, the Yajur Veda, the Sama Veda, and the Atharva Veda, as well as the teachings concerned with phonetics, sacrifice, language, astronomy, etc. Today we would probably refer to it as all theological and secular academic knowledge, concerned as it is with individual and relative truths and incapable of ever leading to the final and highest truth. It can only be realized by a higher knowledge, by what might almost be termed *non-knowledge;* for the language pointing to the object of this higher knowledge in the Mundaka Upanishad is fraught with negatives: ". . . which otherwise cannot be seen or seized, which has no root or attribute, no eyes or ears, no hands or feet; which is eternal and omnipresent, all-pervading and extremely subtle; which is imperishable and the source of all beings." (I.i.6)

The language of Vedantic literature is, of course, not always only negative and vague. There are also a great many positive statements concerning, for example, cosmology, psychology, and the like. It is not always solely phrases like "the inexpressible always remains inexpressible." Yet in spite of all these positive definitions—mainly in connection with the microcosm and the macrocosm—Vedanta is not merely an accumulation of knowledge, a religio-philosophical dictionary from A to Z, but by its very nature and basic tendency also intent on exploding all knowledge, the radical pointer to the "totally other." Vedanta not only leads us into the complexity of outward appearances and into our own inner mental world, but also *out* again: to the "other shore." Like nearly all religions it is primarily a way of salvation, a path of deliverance which takes us from the known to the unknown—which we paradoxically then experience suddenly as the familiar place where we have always been. As far as I am concerned, one may call Vedanta a system; in doing so, however, one should never forget that we are dealing here with a system that in the end cancels itself out.

In this sense Vedanta is above all a spiritual outlook, an attitude of mind, and not so much a closed religion with well-defined doctrines. There is no ceremony by which one "joins" Vedanta. It is true that adherents of Vedanta tend to share certain convictions. Most, for example, believe in reincarnation and the Law of Karma; devote themselves to meditation; believe in the innately divine nature of man, the Atman; and in a transcendental, supra-personal "ground" behind Creation—the latter considered by most as mere *maya* (illusion). Yet nearly all these components also serve as early pointers on the way, inviting us to keep on going; reminding us that "a bridge is for crossing, not for building a house on," as the Persian saying (sometimes attributed to Jesus) goes.

This does not, of course, prevent Vedanta from very often being used as a house. We all know that humans are human, and so-called Vedantins are human too. They often speak their own language, and sometimes, especially in the West, cultivate a distinct elitism. They thus tend to give outsiders the impression of being a church in possession of absolute truth. Particularly those who stress time and again that they are not a church, but merely in the possession of the right key to all religions, often develop a strong missionary zeal. Vedanta then easily turns into an ideology with which to dispatch everything else. A mysterious something called Vedanta then says this and says that. "Vedanta" then knows everything better; in fact "we in Vedanta" are then almost infallible. Still, even the most fanatical Vedantin does not lay claim to true absoluteness, only to a universality, at most, which in no way excludes "the others" but rather includes them—leading then to fear on the part of some Christians of being totally subsumed by Eastern mysticism. The Vedantin can often be quite patronizing because he is convinced that his Vedanta includes all other religions while at the same time transcending them. This attitude sometimes turns into arrogance and not infrequently also accounts for views that are rather superficial. Seeing everything only through Vedantic spectacles, the zealot wants to reduce everything to a common Vedantic denominator. Thus what is unique to other religions—

something one cannot simply appropriate to oneself—is all too often completely overlooked. This is, after all, repeating the bad habits of many medieval Vedanta philosophers who lifted certain sections from the sacred texts, especially from the Upanishads, and forced them to conform to their own particular system. Today's Vedantin often treats the words of Jesus in a similar way. Admittedly, much does fit in with Vedanta, and if a prize were offered for the most universal religious system, Vedanta would have a good chance of winning it. Yet the danger also plainly exists of shaving off the corners of otherness too much, just so that nothing sticks out from the well-rounded Vedantic view of things. Such a way of going about it reveals nothing so much as un-Vedantic doubt in the tenet that in the divine ground all opposites and contradictions cancel each other out. We are often too impatient and would like to achieve this well-rounded perfection here and now, by a little filing here and a little planing there; a process through which, in the case of Jesus, all native Jewish features fly away like so many wood chips and an almost Indo-Aryan guru takes shape, who to our astonishment utters nothing but pure Vedanta wisdom.

Ultimately, one of the natural consequences of Vedanta's universal outlook is more likely to be the humility of non-knowledge. Just as the radical Zen master goes beyond Zen, so the true Vedantin—the one who has arrived at the heart of Vedantic wisdom—in the end no longer knows what Vedanta *is*. More precisely, he is now intimately familiar with what the expression "the end of all knowledge" originally implied. At the highest level all words and concepts disintegrate. In this "poverty of the spirit" the Vedantic mystic finds himself eye to eye with a

Meister Eckhart, a Johannes Tauler, a Zen monk chuck-
ling to himself, a humble Sufi mystic, and probably also an
ancient seer of the era of the Upanishads—who is fortunately still unaware of the later Vedanta schools which
quote him as their authority.

The Spirit of
the Upanishads

NOT ONLY ARE THE UPANISHADS the foundation and start-
ing point of Vedanta, the base, as it were, from which later
Indian thinkers took off in their lofty flights of philosophical speculation; they are, even more so, the wellspring to
which these thinkers like to return again and again to rinse
away the dust of learnedness. The great poetic and illuminating power of many of the passages in the Upanishads
derives its intensity from the same divine source that is also
the aim of all these intuitions of the ardently seeking mind:
the one behind the many, the *Brahman*. To these seers the
Brahman was not an abstract absolute principle but the
Greatest Treasure, the Greatest Good, the Fountainhead of
All Life. The Kena Upanishad says that he is blessed who
realizes Brahman in this life, that not to do so is the worst
misfortune. It was not the intention of the *rishis* (seers) to
construct an impressive intellectual palace to be admired
from without, but within which no one could live; for them
the search for truth was a genuine existential adventure.
Luckily, the texts are still able to communicate to us some-

thing of the radiance on the faces of those whose good fortune it was to realize the limitless Brahman as their own true being.

To a certain extent the Upanishads represent "secret teachings," as the word in fact indicates. Upanishad means "to sit near someone," and here refers particularly to a disciple sitting at the feet of a *guru* (spiritual teacher). In this relationship the teacher, rather than passing on ideas and concepts, directs the disciple's attention to Being itself: he thrusts him into the heart of reality, often only after years of patient waiting. The texts of the Upanishads can, of course, only be the finger pointing at the moon, for they are obviously still dependent on words; yet something of the immediacy and directness of revelation does indeed illumine these words.

The Upanishads are secret teachings to the extent that they point to what eludes the human eye and ordinary waking consciousness. At the more ancient strata of the Upanishads the term refers, above all, to the hidden correspondences between macrocosm and microcosm. While it is still possible for a modern reader to be attracted to those passages for their sheer poetical power, they also not infrequently prove confusing because our modern "scientifically" trained minds are nearly incapable of perceiving those subtle correspondences today. Much there seems to us arbitrarily brought together. We waver between a patronizing smile for these remnants of a worldview full of "magic" and regret that the utter one-sidedness of our own rational-scientific way of viewing things has allowed the organ of perception for those subtle correspondences to atrophy. Goethe's famous lines, "Were the eye not akin to the sun, how could it behold the sun," are unlikely to elicit much more these days than a little "aha-response." We nevertheless seem to be at a turning point today. Awareness of our tragic isolation and longing for a wider context within which man can once again experience himself as part of the universe, not just as its conqueror, is growing steadily. Of course, we can scarcely reestablish in our minds today each and every correspondence as we find it in the Upanishads, but we are becoming more receptive again for the all-encompassing perspective of these sages, one that, on a new level of understanding, it might be possible to combine with scientific reasoning into a new synthesis. The conflict between pre-rational and rational ways of thinking would thus be laid to rest in a higher awareness where the so-called ultimate insights of the Upanishads also have their source.

The real secret teaching of the Upanishads culminates in the much quoted saying *"Tat tvam asi"* ("That [highest divine reality] thou art!"). All else are merely tentative approaches toward this ultimate truth, or preliminary stages where externals are still being linked with externals—as, for instance, the sense organs with various forces of nature and divine essences, however much they may as such already form part of the internal world. Pointing to the existence of a net of relationships is certainly important, but if ultimate identity (not-two-ness) did not also transpire here this network of correspondences would run the danger of becoming an end in itself, an object for hairsplitters to get to work on by extending it further and further—thereby leaving us in the end again with nothing but secret teachings in the plural, with a series of relative truths strung together, with occult mystery-mongering full of conceit for its "knowledge." Although the most secret imaginable insight pertains to the oneness of the Brahman and the innermost Self, this truth is happily also of such brilliant clarity and impact that all occult systems crumble into ruins before it. It is as clear as pure spring water. No closed fist holds anything back here. This truth is by far the simplest and most obvious in the world, even if only very few realize it. Gnostic systems of wisdom as we know them, for example from the Alexandrian realm, have despite their many admirable features often something rigid about them. They tend to hold those who venture into them captive with their knowledge. Esoteric teachings exist which tend to weaken and enslave us to a system, even to our own spiritual vanity. There are other esoteric teachings, the living breath and spirit of which strengthens and liberates us.

Few words in the Christian Gospels more aptly characterize the spirit of the Upanishads than those from the Gospel of St. John, "And you shall know Truth and Truth will set you free." It is a question of *realization,* realization of the kind which no longer binds us to the world of superficial appearances where "the dead bury their dead," but which releases us, includes us in Life Everlasting. To quote a well-known prayer from the Brihadaranyaka Upanishad, and one still much recited by Hindus today: "From the unreal lead me to the Real, from darkness to Light, from death to Deathlessness." (I.iii.28)

Knowledge in Sanskrit is *jnana.* The Upanishads are also referred to as *jnana-kanda,* the portion of the Vedic books dealing with knowledge—in contrast to the *karma-kanda,* the portion dealing with "works" and mainly involving the requirements for ritual. This aspiration on the part of the Upanishadic seers directed solely toward insight and knowledge was no longer concerned with earning a place in heaven for oneself and with propitiating the various deities through ritualistic action and sacrifice. The still very egoic tendencies of the human heart, while they did find full expression in the Vedas, are denounced in the Upanishads. In the light of the new superior knowledge, these urgent human concerns of Vedic times often rather resemble a kindergarten stage of religion. This break with the past is made quite ironically clear in the Mundaka Upanishad, for example, where the old Vedic sacrifice is at first praised but subsequently all the more drastically exposed for its complete futility: "Frail indeed are those rafts of sacrifice and little their merit . . . fools who rejoice in them as the Highest Good fall victim again and again to old age and death. Fools dwelling in ignorance but wise in their own conceit . . . wander about . . . like blind men led by the blind. . . . Immersed in ignorance they flatter themselves, 'We have reached life's purpose. . . .' But in their eager performance of works they do not realize this and fall back when their merit in heaven is exhausted." (I.ii.7–9)

Here profound reflection on the relativity of life as lived, on the shortcomings of all "works," on the chain of cause and effect (also called the Law of Karma), has done away with the childish belief that man can earn for himself an eternal heaven. The new insight proclaims: So long as man is ignorant of who he really is, so long is he tied to the cycle of birth and death, to becoming and ceasing to be. The idea of reincarnation is here taking hold of Indian thinking. It is no longer a secret that even the heavenly realms are finite, mere way stations on the long trek of the individual soul. Once the merit that has earned a man a sojourn in this kind of heaven is exhausted he must again take on a body—until he has realized his true oneness with the Brahman, the divine ground.

Despite this recognition of the ineffectiveness of all

worldly deeds and desires, including the desire for heavenly
bliss, this view in Upanishadic times did not lead at all to a
total negation of the phenomenal world; knowledge and
joy still went hand in hand. Although the naive simplicity of
Vedic times was now lost, the pessimism with which Jainism and Buddhism were to view the world is still far from
making itself felt. The rishi of the Upanishads is not yet the
arhat (an early Buddhist ascetic); he still conceives of the
world as the emanation and overabundance of the divine
Brahman—not as exclusively the consequence of ignorance
and craving for existence. Of course, such a rishi has also
little in common with a contemporary ponderer who does
not know what to make of the world and strains to solve
the riddle of existence. Even if the rishis' insight did not
simply come to them out of nowhere, without any effort—
the many questions and frequent controversies in the texts
show that it did not—they certainly did not resort to reasoning alone. Dürer's *Melancholy* and Rodin's *Thinker*
could be considered as the exact opposite types of the
Indian sage.

REVELATION AND MYSTICISM

The foregoing brings us now, of course, to the problem of
inspiration and revelation, which we by no means find in
Christianity alone. The term *inspiration* should not, however, be overtaxed. If many an orthodox Hindu looks on
every verse of the Vedas and every line of the Upanishads as
the living breath and literal revelation of the highest Brahman, modern man will with some justification be just as

distrustful of such revelatory belief as he is when a Christian claims that every line in the Bible is inspired and of divine origin. Yet the fact that the Vedic books, especially the later texts, the Upanishads, are regarded by Hindus as *shruti,* as what was *heard,* should not be grounds for dismissing it all as ancient superstition. To the Hindu, shruti is what cannot be thought up by the limited human intellect, but is of God. It is what is *forever* valid, never changes, is not dependent on the limited capacity for understanding of any one historical person. The Hindu for this reason is proud not to need a historical founder. The founder and foundation of the Vedas and the Upanishads is the Brahman itself, is what is indestructible and timeless.

This kind of understanding differs somewhat from the belief in revelation of the Israelite peoples. There, a prophet who is quite definitely interested in history and can precisely be located historically, receives a message from a personal God who *speaks* to him. No "God" speaks in the Upanishads, there is only talk of the Brahman, and only few personages there can be considered historical individuals (as can Yajnavalkriya and King Janaka).

Since we in the West are familiar with the concept of revelation almost exclusively from our own Judeo-Christian tradition in connection with the Bible, it never occurred to us that we might be dealing with revelation in Indian religions as well. Christian theological thinking has run something like this: since no "God from on high" makes his presence known to these people, their religion must be a reflection of purely human endeavors, groping attempts of the mind to fathom the Divine Mystery. The wisdom of the Upanishads, and indeed Hinduism itself, was thus branded as primitive religion, as an effort by man to rise above his earthly lot, an effort that could of course never really succeed since it lacked full revelation from God in Heaven.

Anyone who has thought this a comfortable explanation and then chances upon the later commentaries on the Upanishads by the great Vedanta philosophers is probably going to be surprised by the tenacity with which these "scholastics" often end a debate by pointing to the shruti, the revealed scriptures. It is almost like listening to St. Thomas Aquinas, for here, as there, minds strive eagerly to bring revelation in line with reason—yet whenever there is any doubt, the scriptures are made the final authority. One can, of course, interpret the revealed word, even misinterpret it, can try to make it serve one's own particular view of the world; but one must not challenge its authority, for then one becomes a heterodox freethinker—at which point one realizes that imperfect human reasoning is no alternative to biblical belief in revelation.

But we have to get used to the idea that the East has its own concept of revelation. What is important in this connection is not so much the antithesis of personal versus impersonal—since in some of the later Indian texts, such as the Bhagavad Gita, a personal god does speak to man—but the difference between a prophetically revealed religion where ethical precepts receive primary consideration and a mystical religion where man strives above all to *manifest* the divine. The Upanishads belong, without doubt, to this second category; they are mysticism *par excellence*. Their seers are neither prophets in the biblical sense nor philosophers by contemporary standards. Even the term *sage*, that we are so often ready to apply to Eastern mystics, does not quite fit the bill since it gives little indication of the religious intensity of the rishis of the Upanishads. They were certainly sages, but they were also more than that; they were philosophers skilled in debate. Still, we would be hearing little talk of shruti, of "truth heard and seen," if these seers had encompassed truth by means of reason alone. Their experience of the Brahman is more like a *being seized* than the seizing of something, is far more than merely wisdom's ultimate conclusion, and their realization of the Brahman far more than just the last link in a long chain of logical reasoning. The rishis heard and beheld truth directly when they entered a level of awareness in meditation where they became totally receptive. "This Atman cannot be attained by the study of the Vedas, or by intelligence, or by much hearing of sacred books. It is attained by him alone whom It chooses. To such a one Atman reveals Its own form," we read in the Katha Upanishad. (I.ii.23)

Even if this concept of grace is not monotheistic; strictly speaking, the verse clearly shows that what is involved goes beyond human exertion. Not only the personal god of Creation is revealed in the moment of grace but also our own true Self. Grace cannot be "produced." It is possible to work toward that moment by living an intensely spiritual life and throwing off more and more of the encumbrances that hinder us from perceiving truth and becoming free. But at the decisive moment, all "I-ness" still intent on attaining and achieving something has vanished. "I" can only "attain" my true Self when there is no longer an "I" to attain it. Then Atman shines forth of its own. Atman is entirely self-enlightened; it is not enlightened by anything. "When He shines, everything shines after Him; by His light everything is lighted." (Mundaka Upanishad, II.ii.10)

This is not to say that every single sentence in the Upanishads contains ultimate truth in a nutshell and was received in a state of inspiration. There are many tentative beginnings, many a detour; there is much that is couched in legend and anecdote, and there are intense debates, all of which tells more of seeking than finding. Here and there we are probably also dealing with later interpolations, rationalizations, and the like; but what amounts to the quintessence of the Upanishads is not something "thought-up" but a truth "which has come straight from the heart of God," to borrow a phrase from Meister Eckhart (who often comes to mind, as if he were a direct descendant of these ancient rishis).

A LARGER WHOLE

There are over one hundred Upanishads—the sacred number 108 is often quoted—but only the most important ones, those twelve the Vedanta philosophers wrote commentaries to, need concern us here. Their composition is estimated by Western scholars to fall between 1000 B.C. and 600 B.C. This was a period of general awakening: everywhere the human mind was astir seeking answers to fundamental questions; in China as in Greece, in Israel as in India. Karl Jaspers referred to this era of new departures as a turning point in history. Lao-tzu and Confucius in China, the Old Testament prophets in Israel, the pre-Socratic philosophers in Greece, the rishis of the Upanishads, and, following them, Gautama Buddha in India, can be considered the spiritual flowers of this era. Indeed, it seems we are to this day nourished by this time in history as far as our metaphysical heritage is concerned; for no matter how much change and progress mankind has experienced in the external aspects of life, man's real core, his true being, has not changed.

There are probably several reasons why many Indians date their sacred books back to much earlier times than do Western scholars. First of all, being in possession of the oldest revelation in the world tends to enhance self-confidence. Second, since many were circulating long before their final versions were committed to writing it is very difficult to fix these texts historically. They had been handed down orally from generation to generation in the process of which individual families had come to specialize in particular Vedas; moreover, each Upanishad belonged to a particular Vedic tradition. But be that as it may, the precise dating of the Upanishads is of little interest precisely because they deal with what is *timeless*. And if Hindus date them as far back as possible they may do so unconsciously also to heighten awareness of what is everlasting. Indeed, according to the orthodox view the Vedas are not created at all but considered to coexist eternally with the divine, which needs only to breathe new life into them at the beginning of each new cosmic cycle.

The Vedas are the first manifestation of the Brahman, so to speak, are its "word"; and this word is all-encompassing. Visible Creation is little more than the externalization of the word, its coarser form. To the mind of many Hindus, therefore, the Vedas appear to be a world of Platonic ideas of such universality that within it is contained the ideal state of all there is. What cannot be found there simply does not exist at all.

We, of course, tend to see the Vedas more in the light of an evolution in thinking today, that is, not as the finished product of divine revelation somehow descended upon earth at the dawn of time, but as the first poetical expressions and religious intuitions of a human race on the verge of freeing itself from primitive animistic beliefs and gradually and tentatively feeling its way up toward the divine. We already looked at this problem from a somewhat different angle above and concluded that the inner message of the Upanishads, representing in turn the quintessence of the Vedas, can indeed be considered revealed, even if this revelation does not entirely coincide with the biblical concept of revelation. Yet we cannot regard Vedic literature—including, as it does, all kinds of spells, incantations, and such—as pure revelation. But the two approaches—here revelation "from above," there human endeavor "from below"—are not necessarily mutually exclusive. The Vedic books do indeed represent an evolution of human thought over time, the development of *homo religiosus* in tandem with the gradual self-revelation of the divine. However here, unlike in Israel, this evolution pertains less to man's *history* than to his timeless *inner being*, his "heart." "There is in this city of Brahman an abode, the small lotus [of the heart]; within it is a small space. . . . Both heaven and earth are contained within it, both fire and air, both sun and moon, both lightning and the stars. . . ." (Chandogya Upanishad, VIII.i.1–3) We are no longer dealing with revelation concerning this or that deity, but with the fundamental revelation that *all this* is to be found within our own human heart. The Brahman is not only "hidden" in the external world of appearances but also in the Vedic texts—to the extent that they are still provisional and content with partial truths. All Indian mystics agree that at the moment of highest realization the Vedas can be laid aside as useless. "What is peculiar to the Vedas, among all the sacred scriptures, is that they declare again and again that we must go beyond them,"² said Swami Vivekananda. To this should be added, however, that the call to do so occurs actually only at the end of the Vedas, that is, in the Upanishads. They are indeed thoroughly suffused with the spirit of transcendence.

Despite all official bows to their sanctity and ultimate authority, the Vedas no longer seem to play a significant role in the life of the ordinary Hindu. For him the books called *smriti* (what is remembered)—the heroic epics and the popular Puranas, stories rich in myth and legend—are of much greater importance. Even a scholar quoting the Vedas to prove his orthodoxy does so, it seems, mostly as a matter of formality. The Vedas are suffering the same fate as the Brahma Sutras: people celebrate them, continually refer to them, fall down in prostration before them—but no one reads them.

How the Upanishads relate to all that is Vedic and preceded it is not easy to describe. At times an organic transition seems to exist, at other times a radical break—when even a certain sarcasm with respect to the former is not missing. And just as we still find in the Upanishads many traces of the ritualistic portion of the Vedas, so we also find in the earlier Vedic books quite a few germinal ideas that anticipate the wisdom of the Upanishads. Even in the very early hymns of the Rig Veda, we encounter passages of a rather philosophical nature. These are no longer concerned with singing the praises of the numerous nature deities and reaching some kind of heaven, but with knowledge of a higher reality. A good example of this is the *Hymn of Purusha* where Creation is seen as resulting from the sacrifice of man's divine prototype (Ri.X.90); or the *Hymn to Prajapati* where each verse always ends with the question, "What God shall we adore with our oblation?"

(Ri.X.121)[3] This *questioning* becomes still more pronounced in the famous *Hymn of Creation,* which in itself represents a singular great effort to express the inexpressible and break through to the realm where there is "neither being, nor non-being, neither death nor immortality."[4] What at the opening of the biblical account of Genesis is briefly referred to as chaos, as the temporal beginnings of our limited planet earth, so to speak, was in this Vedic hymn interpreted metaphysically as the "state before all time" and included paradoxical statements that are not unlike those in the Upanishads—even reminding us of mystics like Jakob Boehme. What to earlier generations may have appeared as a defect—the hesitant and tentative nature of expression, its continual questioning—we tend to view today in a more positive light. We are tired of all too-ready-made answers. We have had to admit all too often that many a period-bound dogma was just that and, while proclaiming to fathom the mystery once and for all, actually ended up only shrouding it even more. The philosophical and mystical depth of this hymn is unsurpassed; and if everything there still ends in a question, it is not because the light of revelation had not yet shone forth strongly enough, but because questioning is the language most appropriate to the mystery: rather than tying us to the seeming certainty of a finite answer, it frees us for the all-open and inexpressible absolute.

One can almost detect a touch of irony in the last question of this hymn which ends with this verse:

> *None knoweth whence creation has arisen;*
> *And whether he has or has not produced it:*
> *He who surveys it in the highest heaven,*
> *He only knows, or haply he may know not.* (Ri.X.129)

This last question occurs not only in connection with the earliest Indian texts but has actually remained fairly typical right up to the present day for so many ways of the Indian mind, especially as seen in Buddhism and radical Advaita Vedanta. Something almost like disrespect is evident here, the kind that does not even stop short of God the Creator and is not going to rest until it has reached the very foundation of all there is. There are, of course, plenty of theistic systems in India as well (even in Vedanta), where the almighty creator-god, Ishvara, is the last and highest absolute—and it is quite taken for granted that this almighty and all-knowing god knows full well whence his Creation has arisen. Yet there always were, and still are, those other approaches that consider such a god as much too human—precisely because he keeps harping on his omnipotence and omniscience, a circumstance that, especially in Buddhism, has made an absurdity of the creator-god. We are obviously not dealing with a religion of laws, where man is not exactly encouraged by God to ask questions, but with a mystical, metaphysically oriented religion, one that is not easily intimidated by anything or anyone, not even the "Highest Lord in Heaven."

Early germinal ideas anticipating the later Upanishadic wisdom teachings become more pronounced in the Brahmanas, the theological interpretations of the Vedic hymns; but then again, we also find in the Upanishads, as already mentioned, still much that is Vedic. Historically speaking, the Upanishads (with a few exceptions) form the concluding part of what are called the Aranyakas. These texts were studied by the "forest dwellers" and are primarily concerned with the language of symbolic sacrifice and worship. Some of these became part of the Upanishads almost unchanged, some were used more as stepping stones to press onward toward spiritually ever more subtle positions.

SEEKING AND FINDING

Occasionally one or the other reader among those approaching the Upanishads from a purely philosophical point of view might prefer to be given only Upanishadic wisdom's "ultimate conclusions" as expressed, for example, in the form of the *Mahavakyas,* the Great Words. Four such major pronouncements are usually quoted as representing the inner message of Vedanta:

> "Consciousness is Brahman" (Aitareya Upanishad);
> "I am Brahman" (Brihadaranyaka Upanishad);
> "That thou art" (Chandogya Upanishad);
> "This Atman is Brahman" (Mandukya Upanishad).

If we were to content ourselves with such ultimate formulas alone, however, much of the peculiar aura, much of the atmosphere of the Upanishads—their rich "forest fragrance," so utterly at odds with the bookish atmosphere of the proverbial philosopher's chamber—would be lost. Let us not only look at the blossoms or, worse still, preserve them as dried specimens for intellectual home consumption, but let us also consider the rich soil from which they have sprung. Otherwise the celebrated formulas "*Tat tvam asi*" (That thou art) and "*Aham brahma asmi*" (I am Brahman) will become merely handy, and ultimately hollow, concepts to be filed away under the heading "Vedantic wisdom." We must really join those seekers, walk in their footsteps ourselves. Even if those teachers and disciples of Upanishadic times seem somehow primitive to us today, they had one decisive advantage: they were not yet suffering from information glut, they did not yet find themselves assaulted with well-packaged and noisily advertised ideologies, they still had an enormous amount of time and were able to wait and listen. In this the Upanishads also differ from later sectarian developments in India when a solid dogmatism was to leave no doubt as to which was the sole legitimate teaching. The disciple approaching a teacher of one of these dogmatic schools finds himself immediately confined within a closed system. The Upanishads have a beneficial effect because of their unbounded openness, because we are not instantly beaten over the head with deadening dogmas. The disciple's instruction never begins with ready-made formulas; he is given only hints and suggestions. He must seek the answer from within himself. When, after a long time, often spent "only" minding cows, he then returns to his teacher, it is not so much the "correct" answer that matters but the disciple's own immediate experience. It is all right for him to make "mistakes," it is all right for him to be satisfied initially with a mere provisional truth, if to him it is illuminating. The guru seems to trust in the disciple's ability to arrive gradually at the truth on his own—even perhaps ultimately at the highest truth, expressible only by silence.

At times the guru seems knowingly to let the disciple get away with just provisional or even "false" truths. Thus in the Chandogya Upanishad, Prajapati—making his appearance there as something like the prototypical divine teacher—leaves the god Indra and the *asura* (demon) Vi-

rochana initially in the belief that the body is identical with
the highest Self (*Atman*). While Virochana is satisfied with
this materialistic view, Indra soon begins to have doubts
and returns to Prajapati for further step-by-step instruction
concerning the true Self, the Everlasting, the Brahman.
Nowadays we tend to have no time for such long-winded
stories—Indra had to spend 105 years in the state of sacred
discipleship, according to the account there—and as we do
with detective stories, we hurry toward the unraveling of
the puzzling part. But because we did not actually *tread the
path,* we seem to encounter again and again only the same
old familiar clichés. After the first few lessons, every student
of Vedanta philosophy quickly learns not to identify with
his body, nor with his breath, nor with his feelings, nor with
his perceptions, nor with the highest reaches of his intellect,
but with the pure Atman alone, with the true Self enveloped
within these "sheaths." But does he really *know* it deep
down? What the Upanishads are about and emphasize over
and over is the *attainment* of truth, the actual realization of
what all too often was later to become an academic com-
modity.

Thus the student learns step by step that Brahman is not
only *annam* and *prana* (substance and energy) but also
manas (a term that includes the human mind as well as
feelings and volition), *buddhi* (higher intellect and the
power of intuition), and *ananda* (supreme bliss)—and
learning is always understood in its inner sense as a quick-
ening awareness. Although the Upanishads sometimes refer
to the nature of Brahman by a process of negation, as in the
well-known *neti, neti* (not this, not that), this *via negativa*
nonetheless represents only one among many strands in the
fabric of Upanishadic literature. Rather more typical is a
positive ordering by ascending steps of apprehension from

lower to higher levels or stages; but this in no way implies that, once the highest rung of transcendence is reached, the ladder is pulled up to disappear into a totally acosmic absolute. Instead, one so enlightened indeed continues to see the Brahman present in the lower regions of existence, now with even greater clarity than before. In the Taittiriya Upanishad it is expressly stated that food—that is, all physical substance—is not to be despised. Yet this by no means implies that the lofty heights of the later Advaita philosophy with its predominantly negative terminology reflected a totally erroneous development. But before we settle too soon upon those elevated seats from which all Creation is brushed aside as maya, it is useful to begin by joining the ancient teachers of the Upanishads and covering a good distance with them *on foot,* all the while taking deep breaths in the forest air, even with our fleshly, earthly noses.

Admittedly there is also quite a bit of underbrush around for us to stumble over; as noted earlier, no one is really served well by a mere string of abstruse details. But even so, there are also enough verses to inspire us. We may well follow Ramakrishna's advice that when eating fish there is nothing wrong with discarding the head and the tail if we don't care for them. Few religious scriptures probably come without such heads and tails. Still, care must be taken not to carry the cleaning too far, lest in the end nothing remains but a few dry formulas. Without suffocating in the jungle of words, we might as well join in on the debates at the court of Janaka, that most original of sages on a royal throne who rewarded each new fitting answer as to the nature of the Brahman with yet another one thousand head of cattle. We ought to become a bit like children again, children who drive their parents to distraction with their continual

"Why?", always wanting to know what is *behind* this or that phenomenon. Only positivists believe these to be meaningless rhetorical questions. Children know better. In the Upanishads the naive joy in Creation so typical of Vedic times combines in a wonderful marriage with the kind of intense inquisitiveness that causes the surface of phenomena to crack open a bit. Reverence and radical analysis still counterbalance one another. As adults in a modern world we have been so thoroughly purged of childlike wonder and questioning that it is well-nigh impossible for us to transport ourselves back into the world of the Upanishads and its prevailing mood of spiritual pioneering. Today we expect quick ready-made answers of the kind for which we already have a place somewhere in our intellectual cupboards.

BRAHMAN

The word *Brahman,* so central in the Upanishads, is subject to quite a few misinterpretations. While it can be translated as pure or sheer *being* or *the absolute,* this is saying even less than a travel poster says about some Alpine peak when compared to the same peak as experienced by the mountaineer who has actually scaled its cliffs. Even in India intellectualization often went so far as to turn the original meaning of the word *Brahman* (to swell, expand, or increase, from the Sanskrit root *brmha*) into the exact opposite. Brahman then became something altogether static— even Parmenides could not have conceived of it as more static—and was declared the total opposite of maya, which in turn then came in a *negative* sense to embody swelling, giving birth, and dynamic expansion.

A further meaning of Brahman is "sacred word," a meaning derived from Vedic sacrifice. It refers to the mystical power of the words recited by the one offering the sacrifice to cause something to happen. Thus Brahman denoted not so much a deity, such as might in Upanishadic times have gained predominance over all other deities, as the force behind and above all gods which in the first place makes possible every sacrifice, every ritual, and also Creation—itself conceived of as a sacrifice.

Personified as the creator-god, Brahmā (with a long ending) represents a later development, particularly as the first in the *trimurti,* the triad of Brahmā, Vishnu, and Shiva. Yet as high above and beyond all gods as the Brahman is, the role accorded this personal god Brahmā is actually quite humble: hardly a temple exists in his honor; he could never measure up in greatness to Vishnu, Krishna, Shiva, or even the Divine Mother. He usually makes his appearance as their attendant, for instance; or as "the First-Born issued forth from Vishnu's navel"; and, as the "demiurge," is allowed to create the universe anew at the end of each cosmic cycle, an act with which his function is largely fulfilled. In the Upanishads of the middle and later period he is identified with *Hiranyagarbha,* the cosmic Golden Egg, or with *mahat,* a kind of cosmic principle or intelligence emerging from the formless waters and primordial matter that sets in motion the formation of the world. In the Mundaka Upanishad he also appears as the Divine Teacher who passes on his knowledge to his son. In the hierarchy of those Upanishads already strongly under the influence of the Sankhya system, the position of this personified Brahmā

is fixed still below that of *prakriti* (unmanifest Nature).
Only beyond the latter lies the realm of absolute consciousness that is shared by the individual soul.

One should not forget, however, that in the Upanishads,
especially the older ones, there was as yet no clear distinction between a supra-personal Brahman and a personal
creator-god. We do not at all encounter there the kind of
radical distinction between a "higher" impersonal and a
"lower" personal Brahman that the school of Shankara
later undertook to make. The rishis of the Upanishads were
not particularly interested in systematizing, and to them
any sharp distinction between personal and impersonal
would probably have been inconceivable. Compared with
so decidedly personal a creator-god as Jehovah, Brahman
does indeed have more impersonal traits; but it would be
going too far to describe them as totally impersonal. The
Brahman is the potential generating force behind all of
Creation, is what underlies being a particular person, is all-
pervading consciousness behind each individual consciousness, is sheer *being* behind mere being there. The Brahman
of the Upanishads, like the Tao of Lao-tzu, is the best proof
that a rigid, impersonal, cold, and abstract being (the god
of the philosophers) is by no means the only alternative to a
creator-god as understood in the strictly monotheistic
sense. Just like the flexible Tao, the Brahman in its incomprehensible ways animates the barren stretches between
these two extremes and embraces both. It is quite capable
of personification, but withdraws immediately when this
personification threatens to confine it within bounds.

Something of the mysterious magic character of the
Brahman—which, like the Tao, never declares itself
"Lord"—comes across in a story of the Kena Upanishad in

which the Brahman obtains a victory for the gods. In their ignorance the gods immediately boast that this victory was theirs alone. In a gently humorous way the Brahman thereupon teaches them a lesson. When it appears before them, they do not recognize it. Surprised and somewhat irritated, they begin to wonder aloud who this strange, magical being might be. The Brahman then challenges each one of them to demonstrate his special powers; but one by one, each deity has to admit that he is powerless in the presence of this mysterious something. Agni, the god of fire, is not even able to consume a single blade of grass; Vayu, the god of wind, is not even able to bend a tiny blade of grass, much less to carry it off. Prompted by the gods, Indra hastens to find out about this "magic" something. It finally appears to him as a beautiful woman, as Uma, the daughter of Himavat, who now reveals to Indra that this mysterious something has indeed been the Brahman all along.

When we consider the radical separation between the Brahman and the sphinxlike maya in the later Vedanta system of Shankara (about A.D. 800), we are astonished by the degree to which the Brahman had in the Upanishads still something mysterious about it, something even downright mayalike. There the Brahman was still one with its *maya-shakti,* with maya's mysterious creative power that brings forth the universe as well as divine beings. There the Sword of Discrimination, the favorite weapon of later Vedantins, had not yet sundered pure being into two: a static absolute and an "invalid" world of becoming and ceasing to be.

It was long the practice, however, to read into the Upanishads a negative view of the phenomenal world, as Shankara's Advaita Vedanta, for example, characterized it.

Thus Max Müller wrote: "We must bear in mind that the orthodox Vedantic view is not what we call 'evolution,' but 'illusion.' The evolution of Brahman (*parinama*) is heterodox Vedanta, while illusion (*vivarta*), on the other hand, is orthodox Vedanta. . . . To express it allegorically: according to the teachings of orthodox Vedanta the world does not arise from Brahman like a tree from a seed, but like a mirage from the rays of the sun."[5]

Deussen, who read the Upanishads not only through Shankara's eyes, but also through the spectacles of Kant and, above all, those of Schopenhauer, reached similar conclusions. The immense authority which Shankara enjoys in Vedanta has of course led to a situation where his view of the perceived world as maya passes for *the* orthodox Vedanta in many circles; yet this is not really supported by the Upanishads themselves.

Of course, the rishis of the Upanishads, too, were looking for something imperishable and immutable; indeed every religion or metaphysical quest receives its impetus from the thought-provoking phenomenon that all life is subject to change and ultimate dissolution. We search for something that does not die; is not changing all the time; something beyond all transformation; something behind this continual change of scenery. In the rushing stream of events we search for firm ground, for something always present, perhaps a "witness" to all happenings in space and time; we search for an all-seeing eye, an immutable consciousness. But in the Upanishads the immutable is not yet a rigid absolute contrasted with change and transformation; it is itself the *origin* of all change and transformation, all life: it is not only everlasting sheer being, but the eternal creative process itself.

DUALISTIC INFLUENCES

Admittedly traces of the dualistic-pluralistic spirit of the Sankhya system—which distinguishes sharply between a purely passive consciousness (*purusha*) and an exfoliating or "active" Nature (*prakriti*)—had already found their way into certain middle and later Upanishads. In this system there is neither an expanding Brahman, projecting everything out of itself through its generative heat (*tapas*), nor a sovereign creator-god, only a vast number of purely passive spiritual entities, windowless monads, as it were, the purusha. These purusha, which no longer have much in common with the original Vedic purusha, for reasons that are not entirely clear let themselves be drawn into the play of prakriti and sometimes become wholly entangled in its net. The methods of Sankhya and the yoga system connected with it involve freeing from these entanglements each and every one of these purusha until they once again shine forth in their pristine state of pure spirit, which does not even know discursive thought. Discursive thought, in Sankhya, still belongs to the realm of prakriti.

The question of whether the Sankhya system developed within certain Upanishadic circles or entered into the Upanishadic world from without should be one of only academic interest; for however much this philosophy runs counter to the most fundamental tendency in the Upanishads, and Vedanta in general (that is, viewing all as one), it has nevertheless sharpened analytical thinking and brought clarity to many a psychological and cosmological question.

Thus Vedanta took over from the Sankhya system its

systematic step-by-step evolutionary analysis, listing twenty-four principles. First prakriti (unmanifest Nature) evolves into mahat (cosmic consciousness, underlying all individual consciousness), most often identified with buddhi (higher intuition or intelligence) and on the cosmic-mythological plane with the creator-god Brahmā. It is roughly comparable to Plotinus's *nous*. Mahat evolves into *ahamkara* (literally, "I-maker"), the cause of our ego-consciousness and to all Indian sages mischief-maker number one as the root of all illusion, the principal source of all ills. A modern Western writer, Robert Musil, has characterized this "I-maker" very well in his novel *The Man without Qualities*: "We begin to see the interplay between inner and outer; and precisely through knowledge of what is impersonal about man do we begin to discern what is personal about him, such as simple basic behavior patterns like his ego-building drive which, like the nest-building instinct of birds, builds up the ego with whatever materials are available and according to a few simple methods."[6] This ego-building process may be one of the most enigmatic phenomena in the maya-world, which is quite puzzling to begin with. None can deny the existence of this ego; it is impossible to dismiss out of hand its power and obstinacy; and it is particularly troubling for one who desires to make rapid progress on the spiritual path (quite apart from the fact that the desire to make rapid progress is in itself often the product of this ego business). And yet, according to the testimony of many an Indian mystic, this ego is said to dissolve into nothing at the very moment of enlightenment, just as if it had never existed. It is like a thief in a dream who, when finally caught, simply disintegrates at the slightest touch.

From this ego-drive, according to the Sankhya system,

there arises manas (discursive intellect together with emotions and volition). Then follow the five senses (hearing, sight, smell, taste, and touch), the five organs of action, and the five subtle and five coarse elements. Evolution thus works not so much "up" as "down": from cosmic consciousness all the way down to gross matter. We ought to bear in mind here, however, that the highest representative in this hierarchy, that is, mahat, is already a product of prakriti and, therefore, belongs to the "object side" of existence. To these twenty-four principles is then added as the twenty-fifth principle purusha, being the eternal *subject,* remote and unconcerned with the manifold world of prakriti.

While this enumeration (Sankhya literally means "enumerating reasons") came to be absorbed into the Upanishads and Vedanta philosophy, ascetic practice—concerned with ridding the true Self of the dust of transitoriness—also took up many ideas from the world of Sankhya and yoga, although at the time of the Upanishads these were not yet fully established systems. We thus read in the Katha Upanishad: "The Purusha, the inner Self, always dwells in the heart of men. Let a man separate Him from his body with steadiness, as one separates the tender stalk from the blade of grass. Let him know that Self as the Bright, the Immortal, yea, as the Bright, as the Immortal." (II.iii.17) And in the fairly late Svetasvatara Upanishad, which, like the Bhagavad Gita, combines a kind of theism with Sankhya and yoga elements, we read: "As gold covered by earth shines bright after it has been purified, so also the yogi, realizing the truth of Atman, becomes one [with the non-dual Atman], attains the goal, and is free from grief." (II.14)

The insight expressed in this verse is one that all Indian

systems seem to share, namely, the recognition that man's true Self need only be "liberated" by purification, that the highest realization does not involve any addition, but the removal of interfering layers of impurities concealing the True Treasure. Indian thinking here is of one mind with the Greek Platonic idea that self-knowledge is a kind of "remembering," is the rediscovery of what we eternally are.

THE CONVERGENCE OF OPPOSITES

In the Upanishads the ascetic practice of purification is not yet part of a dualistic system in which a static godlike spirit-being is contrasted with a godless world of becoming and ceasing to be. Not even the Svetasvatara Upanishad radically separates the divine from Nature, but despite all Sankhya influences remains true to the fundamental intuitive insight of the Upanishads: "He indeed, the Lord who pervades all regions, was the first to be born, and it is He who dwells in the womb. It is He again, who is born, and it is He who will be born in future. He stands behind all persons and his face is everywhere. The self-luminous Lord who is in the fire, who is in the water, who has entered into the whole world, who is in the plants, who is in the trees—to that Lord let there be adoration." (II.16–17)

The rishis of the Upanishads apparently did not yet see any contradiction in the coexistence of such pantheistic poetry with a systematic way of analyzing away all "natural" sheaths. But is this really so surprising in a living mysticism that proceeds along dialectical lines where every *yes* is followed by a *no* and every *no* by a *yes?* Let us recall the negative language the Mundaka Upanishad employs in describing the imperishable: "... which cannot be seen or seized, has no attributes, no eyes or ears ..." (I.i.6) We seem to be approaching something acosmic here, for what possible *relationship* could there be between such an inscrutable being and our phenomenal world? Are we not already dealing here with the passive purusha of the Sankhya system which has nothing to do with the activities of prakriti? But actually the fact that a barely nameable Brahman can also be related in a positive way to the "womb of all beings" shows that we are here still in an entirely different world of perceptions. The next verse continues: "As the spider sends forth and draws in its thread, as plants grow on the earth, as hair grows on the head and body of a living man, so does everything in the universe arise from the imperishable." (I.i.7)

Such words could equally well characterize prakriti as primordial Nature in its fecund, female aspect, which in Sankhya and several later Vedanta schools becomes something quite distinct from highest divine consciousness. Yet the Brahman of the Upanishads still embraces both pure consciousness and seemingly "unconscious" Nature. The Brahman is the all-encompassing, is what is before and also forever beyond any and all division. It is both purusha and prakriti, at once immutable consciousness and constantly evolving Nature, both the highest transcendental and the underlying ground.

As a result of later developments in religion and philosophy, both in India and in the West, we have become so accustomed to tearing everything apart that it is hard for us now to appreciate this most ancient intuitive insight of the oneness of all that there is. It is considered primitive, that is, still undifferentiated, as though these forest dwellers had simply not known how to use the tools of discrimi-

nation properly. We suspect those who speak of the
"bliss" of Creation—and worse, even of a deity playing a
part in this welling up of Creation—of having most likely
themselves just emerged from the womb of Nature. How
far removed from this, indeed, are the later transforma-
tions of this creative bliss into a *blind Nature* (Sankhya),
a deceptive and enigmatic *maya* (Shankara), a *negative
will* (Schopenhauer), or the distortion into a *will to
power* (Nietzsche)!

In Schelling's philosophy a positive and conscious divine
being is contrasted with an unconscious ground (*Grund*),
here characterized as Nature. This unconscious ground of
Nature has something uncanny about it for many thinkers;
it is even at times close to being identified with evil, or at
least as the source of the possibility for evil. Someone like
Schelling, however, also recognized that the true
absolute—the identity of all existence, even including its
apparent opposites—had to encompass both what is unmanifest and what is of Nature. He was clearly influenced
by Boehme's idea of an unmanifest primal cause (*Un-
grund*), that is, an unchanging original ground not yet split
into contrasting pairs of opposites such as "God" and "Nature," a ground where opposites like light and darkness
cancel each other out. The Brahman of the Upanishads also
constitutes such a *coincidentia oppositorum* (convergence
of opposites). On the one hand, it has all the positive
characteristics of the purusha, such as its transcendent luminous nature for example, making it the aim of all
seekers; on the other hand, it is so broadly conceived that it
also stands for what seems alien, dark, and unfathomable,
such as the expansion of the universe, the unknown forces
of chaos, and the germinal stage of a new beginning. The

Brahman is thus the waters as well as the spirit above them, and also what transcends both.

Although later Upanishads such as the Svetasvatara Upanishad continue to see Nature as divine, a personal god is also beginning to be contrasted there with the ground of Nature. "Know, then, that prakriti is maya and that the Great God is the Lord of maya. . . ." (IV.10) But however much the interpretations of Creation and how it relates to Brahman may differ, we are never in the Upanishads dealing with the kind of conception of Creation we are familiar with from our own Western tradition, that is, as the work of a personal creator-god who brought the world into existence out of nothing, and as an act with a definite beginning and a world with a definite end. In the eyes of the seers of the Upanishads the world was not "made" by a personal creator but *evolved,* "sprung" from the Brahman. For them Creation is a *projection,* a manifestation of the Brahman itself. This is why the Brahman can at some times have more impersonal and at other times more personal traits. What we think of as Creation is the superfluity of the divine and thus to a certain degree "superfluous," but it is still "divine" superfluity. Some passages seem to present the process as though the Brahman actually *transformed* itself into the world of visible phenomena; in other words as though, in a roughly pantheistic sense, it thus *became* the world. It was to remove such misunderstandings from people's minds that Shankara eventually developed his Maya-Teaching, which states that the Brahman only *appears* to become visible Creation, while in reality it continues to abide in itself as the pure absolute. According to this teaching, what we look upon as Creation is an error of perception, an illusion on the part of those who are as yet unenlightened, because there is really only one attributeless impersonal Brahman, the *one-without-a-second*. This continually stressed "without-a-second" means presumably more than anything else without *maya*, without the female prakriti, without even the shadow of a creating activity.

In the Upanishads there was as yet no "second" to be contended with, or to be brushed aside as unreal, because it was still totally integrated in the one Brahman. The basic tenor of the Upanishads with regard to Creation seems to point neither to a crudely pantheistic theory of transformation nor to an interpretation of Creation as illusion. At most one could speak of "emanation" there. Through expressly emphasizing that the Brahman does not exhaust itself in Creation, its transcendental aspect was ensured. The Brahman is absolute *fullness,* transcendent and immanent at once. In the words of the Invocation to the Isha Upanishad: "OM. That is full, this is full. This fullness has been projected from that fullness. When this fullness merges in that fullness, all that remains is fullness."

The kind of speculations and calculations concerning the various cosmic cycles we so often encounter in later Indian texts is nowhere to be found in the Upanishads. Here the focus was on the metaphysical origin of Creation, which is why the question as to whether Creation is a continuous process or a unique event barely surfaced there. In the Vedas we still find the notion that the world was created only once, while at a relatively early stage the view seems to have come to prevail in India that Creation is a process without beginning and without end, that it is only interrupted by periods of cosmic sleep (*pralaya*). This also seems to have been the basic conception in the Upanishads, where teachings concerning the Law of Karma and reincarnation

also already began to appear. It is because the generating
activity of the Brahman is considered something natural
there that it cannot at the same time be considered something unique. Yet what makes for the greatness of these
seers is precisely that they do not get all caught up in details,
that instead of speculating in advance on the future course
of the world, they keep reminding us again and again of the
oneness of all existence: that we are children of immortality, that we come from the Brahman and return to the
Brahman—indeed, that in our innermost being we are always one with the Brahman.

ATMAN

At this point it is appropriate to take a closer look at the
other key term in the Upanishads, the Atman. The difficulty
we have here derives mainly from the fact that on the one
hand the terms Atman and Brahman seem almost inter-
changeable in the Upanishads and that on the other each
has its own history and ambience. And just as we leave
ourselves open to misunderstandings when we translate the
word Brahman simply by "God" or "the absolute," so we
also run the risk of being misunderstood when we simply
render Atman by "soul" or "Self."

According to the teaching of Advaita Vedanta, that is,
the teaching of the one-without-a-second, or non-duality,
the Brahman and our inmost being, the Atman, are identical. But, as we have stressed before, if we want to receive
the illuminating gift of knowledge expressed by "Tat tvam
asi" (That thou art) it is not enough to rely merely on

ultimate concepts; we must try instead to retrace the steps
that led to them.

What happened to the term Atman is similar to what
happened to the term Brahman which, etymologically, suggests a dynamic force and was only later gradually refined
to mean a purely static kind of being. Atman, too, was by its
very nature primarily something dynamic, referring as it
did to respiration as the breath of life, to the very energy
that keeps living beings alive. It was not by accident that it
was originally identified mainly with prana (life energy).
And even if it soon after came to be conceived of as the
imperishable, it was not initially even then thought of as
something static, but as what continually moves and lives,
something we can rely on and the unceasing activity of
which ensures man that he remains alive even when he is
seemingly dead, as in deep sleep or in a faint.

Thus the word *Atman,* like the Greek *psyche* and the
Hebrew *nephesh,* first and foremost stands for breath and
life. But quite early on, the Atman came to be associated
with the individual person, with the "I" or self. It is true
that in later Vedanta the Atman signified almost the exact
opposite of "I" or "ego." But this is so because, there, the
personified "I" is regarded as illusion, and Atman stands
for the divine transcendent Self beyond all ego masks. The
reader of the Upanishads should be prepared to encounter a
considerable variety of meanings, ranging from the simple
human "I" to the divine spirit behind Creation—("He
[the Atman] bethought Himself, 'Let me now create the
worlds.'" Aitareya Upanishad, I.i.1)—to the purusha, the
unchanging background of consciousness beyond space
and time. It is not always clear whether only the "small"
self or the supra-personal, transcendent Self is meant. Later

qualifications, such as *jivatman* (the individual embodied soul still bound to the wheel of birth and death) and *paramatman* (the transcendental Self behind all layers of individuality), are not always helpful in distinguishing one from the other in every single instance. We are dealing with mystical poetry, after all, not with catechisms. Primarily intended is presumably a certain underlying sensation man (and the deity) has when, pointing to his heart, he says, "I." It reflects the inner, subjectively existing man in contrast to the objective world facing him.

That the Brahman and the Atman were actually regarded as one—or more accurately, as *not-two*—can be understood along the following lines of reasoning. In order to pass from the finite to the infinite, a man can take two routes. He can analyze the external world of phenomena and advance step by step toward what is originally behind all appearances. In this way, according to the Vedantic view, he eventually arrives at the Brahman, the foundation of all that there is. But he can also direct his attention wholly inward and analyze the constituent elements of his personality so that step by step, as in peeling an onion, he finally arrives at the reality behind all layers of personality, a reality that can ultimately not really be addressed as "I." What must appear to a normal person as sheer nothing is, for someone who has plunged into this deep level of consciousness reality itself, at once emptiness and fullness. And since there cannot be two entities that are infinite—one behind the macrocosm and one behind the layers of individual personality—the Atman and the Brahman are in the final analysis one. There is but one Atman-Brahman reality.

The mystical paradox, that reality at first seems as if it were nothing, is nicely brought out in the dialogue between

Uddalaka and his son, Shvetaketu, a series of instructions each of which ends with the famous "Tat tvam asi." Uddalaka thus says to his son:

"Bring me a fruit of that banyan tree."

"Here it is, venerable sir."

"Break it."

"It is broken, venerable sir."

"What do you see there?"

"These seeds, exceedingly small, venerable sir."

"Break one of these, my son."

"It is broken, venerable sir."

"What do you see there?"

"Nothing at all, venerable sir."

The father said, "That subtle essence, my dear, which you do not perceive there—from that very essence this great banyan tree arises. Believe me, my dear. Now that which is the subtle essence—in it all that exists has its self. That is the True. That is the Self. That thou art, Shvetaketu." (Chandogya Upanishad, VI.xii.1–3)

At first this sounds like a dialogue concerned with natural sciences and may remind some readers of the passionate search for knowledge of the pre-Socratic philosophers for whom there was almost no difference between a scientific, philosophical, and religious quest. This "subtle essence," imperceptible and yet pervading everything, somewhat resembles Anaximander's *apeiron* or even more tangible primal elements. Anyone who looks at the Upanishads as a whole, however, knows that this "subtle stuff" is only meant here as a pointer toward ultimate reality, or truth, which eludes the grasp of science.

What strikes us is that although the verse begins with an analysis of the outer world it concerns not the Brahman, but the Atman. We would thus do well not to overstrain the above reasoning. That it concerns the Atman demonstrates clearly that the rishis did not see the Self, the eternal *subject*, in man alone but in Nature as well—here as the "spirit" of the tree, so to speak, its indwelling life.

In spite of this interchangeability, however, the Atman and the Brahman have their separate backgrounds and ambience. The Atman always retains something soul-like, psychical and subjective, even when it is recognized and realized as "greater than the Great." It has something of the *spiritus* about it, of the mystic's "climax of the soul," that mysterious point where the finite recognizes itself as the infinite, and at this peak of Self-awareness itself shines forth as the "Light of lights." The Atman is the heart, is what is at the center of Creation and at the same time at the center of each individual: it is the spark and the citadel of the soul. The Brahman has more the character of a divine ground; it can be likened to Meister Eckhart's *Gottheit* (divinity); it is broader in conception than the Atman, more cosmic, more objective. It is possible to approach the Brahman in prayer even without investing it with personal attributes: one can hope to enter the "world of Brahmā." There is no way to pray to the Atman, one can only realize it. In the Brahman one is dissolved; it is like the ocean, whose mighty waves swallow up all, while the Atman more resembles a still mountain lake. Admittedly these comparisons are not of much help, but at least they indicate that we are not dealing with mere intellectual concepts here but with *noumena*, with the "holy" (Rudolf Otto).

When we attribute something soul-like to the Atman, we must nevertheless remind ourselves that despite many similarities it cannot simply be taken as being identical with the Christian idea of the soul. According to Christian doctrine the soul has a beginning—God created it—while the Atman is considered both imperishable and uncreated. As an individual embodied soul, the Atman is like one spark of the divine fire, flickering on from one life to another until it becomes one again with this fire. But Vedanta also holds that the true Self is forever detached from these various lives on earth and all the other manifold forms of existence in the so-called higher and lower regions, that the ignorant, wandering "I" is, as it were, only its shadow, and that it disappears at the moment of enlightenment. "The knowing Self is not born, It does not die. It has not sprung from anything; nothing has sprung from it. Birthless, eternal, everlasting, and ancient, It is not killed when the body is killed." (Katha Upanishad, I.ii.18)

The embodied soul and the higher Self (jivatman and paramatman) are compared in the Upanishads to two birds in a tree. While the one pecks at and eats the fruit of the tree and still remains unsatisfied, the other, the Golden Plumed One, simply looks on. Bewildered and frustrated, the small embodied soul—the little bird hopping around—at last takes refuge with his bigger brother, realizing that his is all the glory. The passage in the Mundaka Upanishad continues: "When the seer beholds the self-luminous Creator, the Lord, the Purusha, the progenitor of Brahma, then he, the wise seer, shaking off good and evil, becomes stainless and reaches the supreme Unity." (III.i.3)

While the soul of the Western Christian tradition is understood to undergo constant change and can even fall and become corrupt, the Atman of Vedanta is understood to be ever-pure and self-enlightened; it is unaffected by one's going astray and no amount of dirt can stain it. It is untouched by space and time, and beyond all superficial personality changes remains forever intact. It is thus like a guarantee that, however much we err and flounder, we never really leave the divine ground. "He indeed is Prana; He shines forth variously in all beings. The wise man who knows Him does not babble. . . . This Atman, resplendent and pure, whom the sinless sannyasin beholds residing within the body, is attained by unceasing practice of truthfulness, austerity, right knowledge, and continence." (Mundaka Upanishad, III.i.4–5) In other words, there is no denying that man must purify himself before he is capable of realizing the Atman; but the Atman itself is not in need of improvement. It neither decreases nor increases. It represents that inner realm where man is forever without fault. "One has a second home," says Ulrich in *The Man without Qualities,* "where all our actions are innocent."[7]

THE FREEDOM OF THE INNER SELF

What is most important to realize is that the Atman can never be made an *object*. Not even God can "do" anything with it. It is the Self as such, the eternal subject, and can therefore also never be "recognized." "Through what should one know That owing to which all this is known?" asks the Brihadaranyaka Upanishad. "Through what, my dear, should one know the knower?" (II.iv.14) It is impossible for that which sees to see itself, for that which knows to know itself. No matter how fast we may swivel around in an attempt to catch our own Self off-guard, we can never capture it. "It is not grasped by the eye, nor by speech, nor by the other senses, nor by penance or good works. . . ." says the Mundaka Upanishad. (III.i.8) Always the point is to look beyond the senses and their functions, which are mere *instruments,* to the real subject, the one that cannot be objectified any more. This subject cannot be dissected or analyzed. It is not accessible to the instruments of the physicist, the chemist, the biologist, or the physician, nor even to the penetrating insight of the psychoanalyst, who will never succeed in getting the Atman onto his couch.

This profound realization produces a feeling of joy and inner freedom: deep down no one can destroy me; my inmost being, the Atman, is at no one's disposal; it is forever free, the servant neither of God nor of any human being. This is why the Upanishads stress again and again that the one who has realized the Atman is fearless.

It has sometimes been pointed out in this connection that speculation concerning the Atman was particularly being advanced in Kshatriya circles, the caste of kings, princes, and warriors. When we remember that intrepid Zen Buddhism met similar favor in samurai circles in Japan, and that Meister Eckhart, who exercised such great influence on the free spirits of his age in Europe, also came from a knightly family, we are led to assume that this can hardly be pure coincidence. While the priestly caste in all religions has always considered it their job to regulate the religious intercourse between heaven and earth, between gods and men— and sometimes did not shrink from keeping people dependent in certain ways—the sages and mystics of the knightly caste frequently aspired to a more direct route to Self-realization and God-realization. When Eckhart speaks of the intangible "something" in the soul, which in his eyes is uncreated, indestructible, and one with the divine ground, he also adds, "Some pastors come to limping over this . . ."

It would be going too far to associate the Brahmins with the business of priestly ritual alone and the Kshatriyas with lofty flights of Atman mysticism. In reality there were innumerable cross-connections, a continual back and forth. We find in the Upanishads nothing to indicate that the Atman teaching was systematically suppressed in Brahmin circles. In fact, the Brahmins assiduously cooperated in the development of this teaching; Yajnavalkriya, perhaps the most important rishi of the Upanishadic era, was a Brahmin. They also did not consider it beneath their dignity to be open to the ideas of the Kshatriyas concerning the true Self. Nevertheless, a certain rivalry between priests and seers cannot be quite rejected out of hand, a rivalry which, in a somewhat different form, also existed in Israel between priests and prophets. In its extreme consequences at least, the Atman teaching is likely to pose a certain threat to any priestly hierarchy that sees itself as God's official representative here on earth, as mediating between "above" and "below."

The seers of the Upanishads seem to have had a sheer limitless aversion to anything in any way limiting. The infinite to them was synonymous with freedom, with supreme bliss. In the Chandogya Upanishad we read: "The Infinite is bliss. There is no bliss in anything finite." (VII.xxiii.1) Or: "What is joy is the space, and what is space is joy." (IV.x.5) Nowhere can the Atman be captured: it is smaller than the smallest thing known and greater than the greatest. "He is my Self within the heart, smaller than a grain of rice, smaller than a grain of barley, smaller than a mustard seed, smaller than a grain of millet; He is my Self within the heart, greater than the earth, greater than the mid-region, greater than heaven, greater than all these worlds." (III.xiv.2–3) The Upanishads keep finding new ways of formulating things in order also to translate into *positive* statements such negatively formulated truths as *neti, neti,* and they do this by means of the provocative language of paradox: "Though sitting still, It travels far; though lying down, It goes everywhere." (Katha Upanishad, I.ii.21)

DEEP SLEEP AND ILLUMINATION

For the rishis a ready analogy for the state of infinite freedom was deep dreamless sleep. In both the waking and the dream state man finds himself in a dualistic world where he is continually up against one boundary or another. But in the state of deep sleep his I-consciousness disappears along with the antagonism between "I" and the rest of the world. There is no longer anything opposing him, no objects, no other human beings. "Where one sees nothing else, hears nothing else, understands nothing else—that is the Infinite. Where one sees something else, hears something else, understands something else—that is the finite. The Infinite is immortal, the finite is mortal." (Chandogya Upanishad, VII.xxiv.I)

These deep-sleep speculations of the older Upanishads[8] have given rise to more than a little confusion. Some have taken this as evidence that the much-celebrated supraconsciousness of the Vedantic sages was really no more than a slipping into unconsciousness, or subconsciousness—something every normal person does quite naturally every night in his sleep without any great meditative effort. It is seen by them as a regression, therefore, a flight from the world and the demands of others whom in dreamless deep sleep one happily need no longer see, hear, or smell. According to these people all this was exacerbated by an accompanying childish sense of omnipotence: I am the center of everything, everything turns around me, I am the whole universe. As it says in the Brihadaranyaka Upanishad, in deep sleep "this [universe] is myself, and I am all." (IV.iii.20)

This is the oceanic feeling, so much ridiculed by Freud, where one presumes oneself to be protected from the harsh realities of life. Moreover, these deep-sleep speculations appeared to lead to totally amoral attitudes. In the Brihadaranyaka Upanishad we read, for example: "[In deep sleep the Atman is] free from desires, free from evils, free from fear. . . . That indeed is His form in which all desires are fulfilled, in which all desires become the Self, and which is free from desires and devoid of grief." (IV.iii.21)

Such passages and similar ones, when taken out of context, have admittedly something alluring about them and can steer people in the wrong direction. Many a yogi contents himself with the lulling of the mind, with the great "yoga sleep." Yet there are also plenty of passages in the Upanishads themselves, in the *Yoga Aphorisms of Patan-jali,* and also in the words of more recent Vedantic sages, that correct such one-sided views. In this century, for instance, Ramana Maharshi has pointed to this problem with particular clarity. "By *mano-laya,* or melting down the dispositions, is meant concentration which temporarily arrests mental activity. As soon as this concentration ceases, mental images, old and new, flow in as usual; and even if this temporary lulling of the dispositions lasted a thousand years, it would not lead to that thorough reduction of mental activity which is meant by liberation or freedom from birth and death. While practicing one must therefore remain alert and inwardly ask, 'Who is having this experience? Who is experiencing this blissful state?' As long as one has not gotten to the bottom of this, one runs the risk of lapsing into a long state of trance, or deep dreamless yoga sleep (*yoga-nidra*). When no suitable guide is available to the practitioner, it sometimes happens that he ends up deceiving himself and falling victim to the illusion of liberation. . . . This is why the practitioner must carefully watch his progress on the spiritual path. He must not fall under the spell of the silenced mind; the moment he succumbs to it, he must rouse his awareness and inwardly ask: 'Who is it who experiences this silence? . . .' The melting down of the mind is a sign that one has come perceptibly nearer the goal, but also the point at which the path divides: one path leads on to liberation, the other to deep yoga sleep."[9] These words echo the often quoted verse in the Katha Upanishad: "Arise! Approach the great [illumined teachers] and learn. Like the sharp edge of the razor is the path, so the wise say—hard to tread and difficult to cross." (I.iii.14)

It is easy to see why, despite such clearsightedness, the state of deep dreamless sleep suggested itself to the rishis of the Upanishads as an analogy. Whenever the mystic has any desire left at all to communicate something, he cannot but resort to analogy. Even for us today, sleep remains a necessary means of recovery from the turmoil of a complex and noisy phenomenal world—its many contradictions and squabbles pursuing us even in our dreams. It is not surprising, really, that so-called primitive people believed that one asleep had "gone to his everlasting home," that is, had become one with the divine, and must not be wakened lest he not find his way back to himself. Some elements of this rather animistic imagery might also have found their way into the older Upanishads.

Later, the Mandukya Upanishad, in particular, points to

the relativity of deep sleep. According to this Upanishad there is still a fourth state, called *turiya,* beyond the three relative states (waking consciousness, dream, and deep sleep). Strictly speaking, this is not still another state, however, but constitutes the true state we find ourselves in at all times, even if we are unaware of this; while the other states end when one takes over from the other. The analogy of deep sleep is thus also only like a finger pointing to the Atman, not the Atman itself, which remains concealed behind the veil of blissful ignorance, or *ananda-maya.* One can perhaps understand why the rishis of the older Upanishads, in their first attempts to communicate their experiences, often described them as though pure bliss was already synonymous with ultimate reality itself. We should also consider the possibility that what for many of us is little more than sinking into a state of blurred consciousness, may for these mystics actually have been a journey through illumined territory, so that for them sleep could sometimes quite naturally have become a symbol for the realm of the divine. Thus we read in the Chandogya Upanishad, for example, that the bridge (or dam) between the waking world and the world of deep sleep is not crossed by day and night, nor by old age, sickness, or death. "All evils turn back from It, for the world of Brahman is free from all evil. Therefore, having reached this dam, he who is blind ceases to be blind, he who is miserable ceases to be miserable, he who is afflicted [with disease] ceases to be afflicted. Therefore, having reached this dam, the night becomes day; for the World of Brahman is lighted once and for all." (VIII.iv.1–2)

A great many verses refer to the "light" of the Brahman-Atman reality that enlightens mankind—that indeed is always shining within man. "There, the stainless and indivisible Brahman shines in the highest, golden sheath. It is pure, It is the Light of lights; It is that which they know who know the Self." (Mundaka Upanishad, II.ii.9) Then there is the verse in the Svetasvatara Upanishad whose jubilant, affirmative tone captures, so to speak, the quintessence of Indian mysticism: "I know the great Purusha, who is luminous, like the sun, and beyond darkness. Only by knowing Him does one pass over death; there is no other way to the Supreme Goal." (III.8)

This luminous transcendental reality may sometimes appear to be the "totally other"—we find frequent references to the "other" shore beyond darkness; but the rishis of the Upanishads were in fact concerned to show that we too are this light. Nowhere is this made more clear than in the following verses from the Isha Upanishad: "The door of Truth is covered by a golden disk. Open it, O Nourisher, lone traveler of the sky! Controller! O Sun, Offspring of Prajapati! Gather Your rays; withdraw Your light. I would see, through Your grace, that form of Yours which is the fairest. I am indeed He, that Purusha, who dwells there." (15, 16)

On the surface this verse is primarily about the importance of perceiving the real god behind the disc of the sun. God is asked to take off his "natural" mask—the disc visible in the sky—and reveal himself to the one praying. A Christian theologian might say that deep within the heathen's worship of the sun flickers the longing for the true God.

However, these verses also lead us deeper and directly into the heart of Vedanta; for insofar as "God" remains only the "other," the one who blinds us earthlings with his divine light, he is lastly a "golden disk" concealing the absolute ground where God and man are one. Thus even the luminance of divine omnipotence is still a form of maya. This veil, too, must drop away before the knowledge can come in a flash: *That I am.* This verse is reminiscent of Meister Eckhart's praying to God that God may "quit me of god"—to enable him to enter eternity.[10]

"Totally other" and inmost immanence come together here. The urge to conceive of the beyond as always further beyond goes hand in hand with the knowledge that it is right *here.* "What is here, the same is there; what is there, the same is here. He goes from death to death who sees any difference here," we read in the Katha Upanishad (II.i.10). In a dualistic world we are subject to the laws of becoming and ceasing to be, and must always pay for our wrong views by being subject to the round of death-and-rebirth. In duality and plurality fear always reigns; but he who has realized non-duality has overcome fear, the knots of his heart are untied (an image occurring repeatedly in the Upanishads), and he has escaped the clutches of death. "He who knows the supreme Brahman . . . he overcomes grief; he overcomes evil; free from the fetters of the heart, he becomes immortal." (Mundaka Upanishad, III.ii.9)

BRAHMAN SEEN WITH EYES OPEN

In the Upanishads the oneness continually being attested to is still open in all directions. It can take on pantheistic and acosmic or even theistic shades. Although "earless," the Brahman has "a thousand ears" with which it hears. The spirit pervading the universe, just celebrated as formless, can in the next verse take on form again: "Thou art woman, Thou art man; Thou art youth and maiden too.

Thou as an old man totterest along on a staff; it is Thou
alone who when born, assumest diverse forms." The im-
ageless and formless becomes transformed into poetic imagery of the highest order, the poet-seer thereby mimicking
the activity of the divine. "He, the One and Undifferentiated, who by the manifold application of His powers produces, in the beginning, different objects for a hidden
purpose . . ." says the poet of the Svetasvatara Upanishad,
and continues: "Thou art a dark blue bee; Thou art the
green parrot with red eyes; Thou art the thundercloud, the
seasons, and the seas. Thou art beginningless and all-
pervading. From Thee all worlds are born." (IV.1, 3, 4)

What was most important to the seers of the Upanishads
was to experience the Brahman's omnipresence and non-
dual nature everywhere and at all times. The deep-sleep
speculations and statements about absorption are only the
negatively worded expressions of this experience, in which
the Brahman seems like "sheer nothing," like an "emptiness," something beyond the known and the unknown. To
quote from the Kena Upanishad: "The eye does not go
thither, nor speech, nor the mind. We do not know It; we
do not understand how anyone can teach It." (I.3) Yet what
looks like radical agnosticism here, or a variation of the
Buddhist silence with respect to the ultimate truth, immediately turns into positive assertions again about this experience. Brahman is not only emptiness, it is also absolute
fullness. The negatively expressed experience, that is, that
one sees nothing "else"—because nothing is actually *there*
to be seen—turns into the assertion that in the world
around us, too, nothing *else* really exists: the world must
simply be seen at a more *fundamental* level. "The wise man
beholds all beings in the Self, and the Self in all beings; for
that reason he does not hate anyone. To the seer, things

have verily become the Self: what delusion, what sorrow, can there be for him who beholds that oneness?" (Isha Upanishad 6, 7) In a certain sense the one awakened, the one enlightened, is also "alone" precisely because he is one with all other beings; because he experiences himself as the Brahman, as the one-without-a-second, all-pervading—indeed he *is* at bottom everything. "That immortal Brahman is before, that Brahman is behind, that Brahman is to the right and left. Brahman alone pervades everything above and below; this universe is that Brahman alone." (Mundaka Upanishad, II.ii.11)

THE MYSTIC SYLLABLE OM

The best-known and most important word symbol for Brahman is OM or AUM. It is the alpha and omega. Just as the mouth opens for the A, so the process of creation is opened by this word. It is then maintained by the U, and comes to a close with the M. Similarly AUM (in pronunciation contracting to OM) symbolizes the three relative states of waking, dreaming, and deep sleep. Yet beyond these, OM also has a fourth, a soundless aspect. In this aspect it symbolizes the absolute silence from which the word is born.

Many passages in the Upanishads refer to this archaic cosmic word with the greatest reverence. In the Katha Upanishad we read, for instance: "That which you see as other than righteousness and unrighteousness, other than all this cause and effect, other than what has been and what is to be—tell me That. . . . The goal which all the Vedas declare, which all austerities aim at, and which men desire when they lead the life of continence, I will tell you briefly: it is

OM. . . . This syllable OM is indeed Brahman. This syllable is the Highest. Whosoever knows this syllable obtains all that he desires. . . . This is the best support; this is the highest support. Whosoever knows this support is adored in the world of Brahma." (I.ii.14–17) OM is the bridge, the link between the relative and the absolute, between a lower and higher being. It prevents the relative phenomenal world from being seen merely as the result of the inexplicable fall from the absolute, as a complete break from it. In its transcendental aspect OM is the absolute itself; it is that fourth state (turiya) which in the Mandukya Upanishad is almost exclusively described in negative terms. "It is not that which is conscious of the inner world, nor what is conscious of the outer world, nor that which is conscious of both, nor that which is a mass of consciousness. It is unperceived, unrelated, incomprehensible, uninferable, unthinkable, and indescribable." In positive terms it is then called "all peace, all bliss, and non-dual. . . . This is Atman and this has to be realized." (7) Just as plurality disappears in the absolute aspect of OM, so from the divine sound OM it reemerges. All we see and hear are the manifestations of this one primeval vibration OM. If we dwell on this word in meditation, we are brought from plurality back to unity—Logos gathers in again what was scattered in order to lead us toward that state of unique peace which surpasses all comprehension. In the Mundaka Upanishad we read: "Take the Upanishad as the bow, the great weapon, and place upon it the arrow sharpened by meditation. Then, having drawn it back with a mind directed to the thought of Brahman, strike that mark, O my good friend— that which is the Imperishable," and: "In Him are woven heaven, earth, and the space between, and the mind with all the sense organs. Know that non-dual Atman alone and give up all other talk. He is the bridge of Immortality," and: "He moves about, becoming manifold, within the heart, where the arteries meet, like the spokes fastened in the nave of a chariot wheel. Meditate on Atman as OM. Hail to you! May you cross beyond the sea of darkness!" (II.ii.3–7)

We are deep in the heart of the Upanishads here, where the cosmic and the supra-cosmic join as in marriage with the individual and the very small. Again and again we come across these two basic trends: the infinite becomes the word, thus taking root in the human heart, and what is inmost in the heart expands as man leaves his "I" behind and bounds across to the "other shore." Seen from the absolute point of view he does not, of course, move an inch from the spot, just as the infinite never *sets out* to become finite. Yet the religious life would be no *life* if it consisted merely in constantly pointing to certain fixed and lifeless truths in the plural. The size of the small "thumb-sized" Atman in the heart and of the "endless" sea of the Brahman may be fixed, but by relating one to the other the whole thing suddenly takes on life: the Atman is smaller than the smallest mustard seed, yet larger than all the worlds. We are reminded of the mustard seed Jesus equated with the Kingdom of God because it grows to become a huge tree. We begin to develop a sense for what living religion really is: to die and become, to grow and to realize—not just holding to be true some eternal articles of faith.

MYSTICISM AND ETHICS

While other Hindu texts, such as the Laws of Manu, regulate the ethical conduct of the Hindu down to the minutest detail, the Upanishads, being mystical writings, are under standably interested in ethical principles only insofar as they serve the attainment of final realization. This realization or supreme enlightenment discloses to the seer's inner eye a "Kingdom of God beyond good and evil." However, only those who have left behind darkness and evil are able to reach this kingdom. The problem is the distracting scatteredness of the world—the negative aspect of diversity—which is no longer perceived at the most fundamental level as emanating from the One, as the generative unfolding of the Brahman, but only in terms of this or that individual manifestation. "He who, cherishing objects, desires them, is born again here or there through his desires. But for whom those desires are satisfied and who is established in the Self, all desires vanish even here on earth," says the Mundaka Upanishad. "This Atman cannot be attained by one who is without strength or earnestness or who is without knowledge accompanied by renunciation. But if a wise man strives by means of these aids, his soul enters the Abode of Brahman. . . . A Rik-verse declares: This Knowledge of Brahman should be told to those only who have performed the necessary duties, who are versed in the Vedas and devoted to Brahman, and who, full of faith, have offered oblations . . . and performed the rite, according to the rule. . . ." (III.ii.2–4, 10)

In other words, the wisdom of the Upanishads, like any truly esoteric knowledge, should not be "cast before swine." However thoroughly the relative opposites of good and evil will eventually be transcended, a morally immaculate life is always a precondition. We usually find these moral admonitions at the end of an Upanishad. It seems as though only at the end of their lofty mystical flights had it suddenly occurred to these seers that it might perhaps not be enough to take ethical conduct for granted without a word on the subject. In some cases we might also be dealing with later additions and interpolations. These words form the shell, as it were, to protect the delicate core, the Mystic Treasure. They also serve to set a few things straight, especially what may be open to one-sided interpretation or misuse. Conversely, these admonitions are held in check by what precedes them, so that whatever protection they afford is not going to smother the mystic flame. If, for example at the end of the Mundaka Upanishad, a certain piety and "book knowledge" (of the Vedas) are insisted upon, one needs only to flip back a few pages to find a passage making it crystal clear that the Atman *cannot* be realized by works, nor by the study of the Vedas, nor by intense cerebration. In the end all human effort is left behind to make way for the moment of grace.

The ethics of the Upanishads bear the imprint of mystical dialectics. Man can not become one with the universe until he becomes "nothing," until he "un-becomes." In the Maitrayani Upanishad we read, "His self abiding in the Self, he is infinite and not supported by anything." (6, 20) Let us remember that for the rishis of the Upanishads true bliss meant limitless expanse, boundlessness. Yet they achieved this limitless expansion only through limitless renunciation. "All this—whatever exists in the universe— should be covered by the Lord. Protect the Self by renunciation. Lust not after any man's wealth," says the first verse of the Isha Upanishad. The commandment or prohibition here is not in the nature of a threatening "thou shalt not"; what is much more important is the other side of the coin: the blissful joy resulting from such renunciation. The ultimate goal is and remains *ananda,* joy, bliss, and happiness in God. Total renunciation leads to total compensation through the discovery of "the true form of his proper being" (Heinrich Zimmer) concealed all along behind those outer manifestations man has been so preoccupied with. To the enlightened, *everything* tastes of God, as Meister Eckhart put it. And like the seer at the end of the Taittiriya Upanishad he can declare, "I am food, I am food, I am food! I am the uniter, I am the uniter, I am the uniter! I am the first-born of the true, prior to the gods and the navel of Immortality.... I am radiant as the sun." (III.x.6)

The Upanishads are neither premoral nor amoral—and certainly not immoral. They are above morals; that is, they see all morals and ethics only as a springboard to the other shore, not as an end in itself. Anyone who finds the Upanishads lacking in compassion for our fellow man should not on that account give up on them—even less strain to find there pronouncements of passionate brotherly love (*agape*). A measure of healthy concern for one's fellow man, expressed especially in the deep respect shown every guest, was presumably enough for them. The Upanishads belong to jnana literature, a literature intended as a guide to the highest knowledge beyond any purely intellectual understanding. They enable us to look right into the heart of Creation and the nature of the divine, only in a way different from the Christian Gospels. There is no scripture in the religious literature of the world where *all* aspects are given equal prominence. But whether we live in the West or the East, nothing really prevents us from combining the wisdom of the Upanishads with the Christian impulse of an engaged love for our fellow man, just as no one is stopping us from complementing the joyous message of love with wisdom gleaned from the Upanishads.

JOB AND NACHIKETA

The Upanishads are for us today above all a lesson in fearlessness. Man is not overwhelmed and crushed by an almighty and distinctly male god there, but, sword in hand, forges ahead on his own until he has pushed open the last doors to the unknown. It seems by comparison like nothing so much as divine sarcasm when the Old Testament Jehovah, appearing to the suffering Job in a storm, says to him, "Gird up now thy loins like a man; I will question you, and you tell me the answers." After all, Jehovah does not really want to converse with Job, still less be informed by him; he does not even regard him as an equal, but as a servant whom one orders around until he falls silent. Indeed, Jehovah knows full well that Job cannot give any answers to his questions. "Where were you when I founded the earth? Tell me, if you have understanding," comes the voice from the clouds. (38.2–4) Job is not a Meister Eckhart who could say: "In my eternal birth, however, everything was begotten. I was my own first cause as well as the first cause of everything else. If I had willed it, neither I nor the world would have come to be! If I had not been, there would have been no god. There is, however, no need to understand this."[11]

Jehovah would no doubt have been astonished at this rather Vedantic-sounding reasoning on the part of the Dominican monk. The battle—the struggle between God and man—would probably also have been less one-sided if Nachiketa, the hero of the Katha Upanishad, had been facing God, in place of Job. Not without an undertone of cynicism Jehovah asks Job, "Have the gates of death been

shown to you, or have you seen the gates of darkness?"
(38.17) As for Nachiketa, he presses on to meet the god of
death. He does not rest until he has revealed to him the
ultimate answers concerning life and death and, beyond
these, reality itself. When Yama promises to grant him
many sons, grandchildren, herds of cattle, and the like, if
only he will forgo answers to such ultimate questions,
Nachiketa does not let himself be put off by such offers of
temporal possessions. Presumably he does not wish to die
like Job, "old and full of years," but would prefer to die
young but enlightened. "But, O Death, these endure only
till tomorrow," he says to Yama. "Furthermore, they exhaust the vigor of all the sense organs." (I.i.26) On the
surface, this dialogue between Nachiketa and Yama seems
to concern only the question of whether or not there is life
after death. But as it continues we learn that it is not at all
only about continued existence after death—indeed not
even about attaining some kind of heaven, which falls, after
all, still within the realm of desire and thus what is finite—
but about knowledge of the ultimate truth. "That which
you see as other than righteousness and unrighteousness,
other than all this cause and effect, other than what has
been and what is to be—tell me That," says Nachiketa,
thereby posing the questions typical of a follower of jnana
who, with sword drawn, intends to slash through the veil of
maya. For one enlightened, distinctions and contradictions
no longer exist. He is "he to whom Brahmins and
Kshatriyas are mere food, and death itself a condiment." By
rising above, or as it were, "eating up" all duality and
distinction, he also "rises above the gates of death"—death
ruling only in the realm of duality. The kind of immortality
he thereby gains is not mere continued existence in a quan-
titative sense (an existence ultimately not likely to escape

the shadow of death) but life eternal which, in its "thusness beyond all opposites," can no longer be expressed in words. "Who, then, knows where He is?" (I.ii.14, 25)

As we said earlier, the Upanishads are part of a mystical wisdom literature, not of scriptural prophesy. Still, I would like to conclude this chapter with a line at the end of the Svetasvatara Upanishad which has a prophetic ring to it: "When men shall roll up space as if it were a piece of hide, then there will be an end of misery without one's cultivating the Knowledge of the Lord." (VI.19–20)

Krishna the Omniscient: The Message of the Bhagavad Gita

THERE HAS NEVER BEEN a lack of praise. The Bhagavad Gita, often referred to simply as the "Gita," is a tiny fragment of the giant epic the Mahabharata, and has often been extolled as the jewel of Indian literature; as the Hindu "Bible"; as a brilliant synthesis of all the important religious and philosophical currents of India; as the reconciliation of jnana and *bhakti* (the Path of Knowledge and the Path of Devotion to God); and finally as the Song of Selfless Action, giving courage to a Gandhi, even while in prison. Few great yogis or scholars in India could pass it over without writing a commentary on it.

Yet there has also never been a lack of criticism. There is talk of too much eclecticism, of an all-too-colorful mix of divergent currents of thought which, so it is said, cannot really be so easily brought together under one common denominator; internal contradictions are supposedly only papered over, not really reconciled. The suspicion has also been voiced from time to time that too many authors may have been at work on it in the course of time, so that it is now nearly impossible to disentangle the true, original Gita from all the later sectarian additions. Other voices complain that the Gita opens with a dilemma, not just for the hero Arjuna, but also for the modern reader: the problem of war. Pacifists and followers of passive resistance, who like to point to the Indian teaching of non-violence (*ahimsa*) as the basis for their beliefs, are thus said to be troubled by the opening verses, despite their great admiration for many other passages in the Gita.

The position of the Bhagavad Gita within orthodox Hindu literature is also somewhat ambiguous. As part of the Mahabharata epic, it no longer belongs to the sacred Vedic books, no longer to shruti (revelation), but to smriti (remembrance), a word referring particularly to those texts where eternal truths are clothed in mythological and historical garb—like the Ramayana, the Mahabharata, and the Puranas—and thereby made more popular. In actual religious practice, however, the Gita is usually regarded as direct divine revelation and its authority is rarely doubted. It most certainly plays a much greater role in the everyday life of the Hindu than do the Vedas. Public readings of the Gita are still quite popular in India today, and the Gita is probably the most widely read book of the Hindus in the West as well.

The high place the Gita occupies in the edifice of Vedanta has never been disputed. Together with the Upanishads and the Brahma Sutras it forms the threefold foundation of Vedanta. But when seen in terms of a subtle ranking order, the situation is rather the reverse from what it is in popular Hinduism. In Hinduism the Gita exercises without any doubt a much greater influence than do the Upanishads, while a strict Vedantin (particularly a follower of Shankara) will probably give higher priority to the Upanishads. These were and remain the true "Ved-anta": they constitute the original Vedantic revelation, they have the greater *impact* (even noticeable to the ear when listening to the Sanskrit versions being chanted), and they are both more ancient and in a certain sense also more radical. Many passages of the Gita, on the other hand, seem more rounded, more polished. It is already the product of a later age, however early. It is a sort of catchment basin for many different currents of thought where modern Hinduism (especially Hinduism as characterized by theism) and the Vedic age meet about halfway.

For all its maturity and roundedness the Gita is no tired work of old age. It also goes far beyond mere artificial syncretism. If besides its well-roundedness it did not also possess freshness and youthful vigor, it would hardly still inspire us so much today. Despite this and that later addition it is no mere patchwork, but indeed an organic whole the totally universal perspective of which has saved many a reader who chanced upon this little book from the narrowness and despair of an apparently meaningless life, luring him on toward the immeasurable expanse of the realm of the divine. There will, of course, always be those who, in a somewhat ill-humored way, approach such books only in order to poke around in them to pick out "contradictions" like so many burnt bits of onion and bacon in an otherwise splendid breakfast. But anyone who integrates the study of the Gita into his daily religious life—who lives by it—will soon notice that these so-called contradictions only reflect the multidimensional levels of existence, both human and divine. In the Gita's universal view of things everything has its place. Its principle is all-inclusiveness. Doing away with the either/or approach, it proclaims the typical Eastern view of things: "this-as-well-as-that," without thereby losing any of its seriousness and depth.

The powerful impact the Bhagavad Gita has on so many people has without question also much to do with the pronouncements of its hero, Shri Krishna. We will not go into a historical discussion about this figure, nor engage in a theological debate concerning his divinity. We just want to be attentive to the voice that speaks here. Whether or not we believe, as orthodox Hindus do, that Krishna stood there on his chariot on a specific day in time and delivered this exact message to Arjuna in precisely those words (in verse!), we will probably have to admit that there are very few sacred texts where the voice of the divine reaches us so clearly and directly, and with such self-evident authority. A human poet has, of course, composed the Gita, and later generations have had a hand in it. Yet we do not have the impression that we are dealing here only with examples of human imagination and inventiveness, with love of philosophy having had a field day, so to speak. Certain observations and attitudes are necessarily dated and could be found in many other human folk epics, and thus do not necessarily require divine authorship; but in numerous instances the voice does come clearly from "above," and with tremendous assurance—sometimes more from the head, sometimes more from the heart, and sometimes more from the gut of the eternal God, appearing disguised here in the figure of Krishna.

A God of War?

Even for the author of this study there remains the stumbling block at the beginning of the Gita: war and the call to battle. We could make light of it and say that the subject really has nothing to do with Vedanta philosophy as such, that Vedanta, as we all know, is concerned with timeless metaphysical principles, not with the din of history's battles. But in doing so we would be denying Vedanta any practical relevance and be escaping into the realm of abstraction; but above all, we would not be doing justice to the spirit of the Gita, which is, of course, not just a series of practical instructions but also a philosophical didactic poem. Yet it is not just by chance that the highest truths about being, for the most part already present in the Upanishads, are revealed here on the battlefield of life, rather than in the solitariness of the forest retreat. This is not only so because the Gita happened to be placed at the precise spot in the Mahabharata epic where the war between the Pandavas and the Kauvaras is about to begin. Although through his arguments Krishna takes his friend Arjuna (and with him his listeners and the reader) far beyond the earlier problem of war—so far indeed that it is often lost sight of altogether—the problem still remains the point of departure, the point of reality where all questioning in the Gita begins.

The Gita does not solve the problem of war: rather it thrusts us right into the heart of the problem of war, *any* struggle, and shows us by means of one example how easily in actual life we can be drawn into tricky situations and conflicts of conscience the likes of which hardly arise for the ascetics in forests and caves. Krishna, in the Gita, is not addressing a *sannyasin* (a monk; one who has completely renounced worldly life), but a member of the warrior caste who still finds himself right in the midst of life. Yet even if much of his message is universal and forever valid, he is also speaking at a specific time in history when war as a means of imposing a "just" (and often less just) solution was hardly ever called into question in Eastern and Western civilizations alike. It is therefore all the more significant that in spite of Krishna's unyielding exhortation to battle, war is already shown here in terms of its questionable aspects. At the end of the war Arjuna's doubts (and even more so those of Yudhishtira who appears as the embodiment of *dharma*, the "correct way," in the Mahabharata epic) turn out to have been justified to a degree, even though the cause was "just": the war throws the country back into barbarism for a time, losses on both sides are enormous, and in the face of all this devastation the question justifiably arises as to whether this war, lastly, made any sense at all. There are no cheap attempts at painting things black and white in the Gita: no heroes in the service of the good cause and bad guys in the service of the devil and the ending a triumphant victory of good over evil. A certain dualistic pattern, however, is evident in Krishna's pronouncements, the kind we find in almost all religions: the struggle of light against darkness, against *asuric* (demonic) forces. He says himself that he manifests himself anew in every age "whenever there is a decline of dharma ... for the protection of the good ... for the destruction of the wicked ..." (IV. 6–8) But we should keep in mind that his ethical attitude is embedded in a worldview where gods (*devas*, literally "luminous beings") and dark powers (*asuras*, "demonic spirits") are regarded as relations, as "cousins." Both are aspects of the one divine reality, the Brahman, which is, above all, pairs of opposites. Good and evil are relative. It is not easy to draw a clear line between them on the larger scale of things, and even more difficult to do so on the battlefield. Arjuna sees many relatives and friends in the enemy camp and it is precisely this circumstance which causes him, like a wavering Hamlet, to lower his weapon even before the battle has begun. The world is not neatly divided here in two halves. It is shown in all its ambiguity, in its condition as maya, where all good contains a little evil and all darkness a little light. This is a fratricidal war, and one needs only transpose this conflict to our own times to become aware of the complex problems involved in declaring one part of mankind (or even one part of one's own country) as the other side, as "them." Fortunately, few people today still know how to extricate themselves from a dilemma by means of a couple of smart slogans. Only very few, I hope, hold it against Arjuna that he had second thoughts and did lower his weapon. We are almost as grateful to him for hesitating as we are to the divine Krishna for his subsequent explanations which, although enabling us to have a certain insight into the ultimate mystery of the divine as well as our own true being, in the end do not really provide a quick-and-easy solution to the concrete problem of war.

By the end of the second chapter Krishna has already raised his friend Arjuna to a level far above the hustle and bustle of the politics of the day with his religio-philosophical reflections concerning the true nature of man. Some will breathe a sigh of relief: thank god we are rid of these problems! Now we can get on with our metaphysical and spiritual discussions. And as Krishna bestows his benevolent smile upon his friend and disciple Arjuna, it does indeed seem as if all pros and cons had vanished like so many phantoms. Yet anyone looking closer will find enough strands tying what is actually happening here to the realm of truth eternal. "You have been mourning for those who should not be mourned for; yet you speak words of wisdom," says Krishna. "Neither for the living nor for the dead do the wise grieve. Never will there be a time when I do not exist, nor you, or these kings of men. Never will there be a time hereafter when any of us shall cease to be. Even as the embodied Self passes, in this body, through the stages of childhood, youth, and old age, so does It pass into another body. Calm souls are not bewildered by this." (II. 11–13)

Then, going beyond all individuality, this: "The unreal never is. The Real never ceases to be. The conclusion about these two is truly perceived by the seers of Truth. That by which all this is pervaded know to be imperishable. None can cause the destruction of that which is immutable. Only the bodies in which the eternal imperishable Self is the indweller are said to have an end. Fight, therefore, Arjuna. He who looks on the Self as the slayer, and he who looks at the Self as the slain—neither of these apprehends aright. The Self slays not nor is slain." (II. 16–19)

And after having gone on to extol the indestructibility of the Atman, Krishna, in words quite similar to those we find in the Upanishads, adds: "But if you think the Self repeatedly comes into being and dies, even then, O mighty one, you should not grieve for it. For to that which is born, death is certain, and to that which is dead, birth is certain. Therefore you should not grieve over the unavoidable." (II.26–27)

Put in more systematic terms we could say that Krishna presents three arguments here:

1. Sheer being connecting and pervading everything cannot be destroyed by anything or anyone. It is the source of all change but is itself unchangeable. It is also the transcendent, absolute aspect of man, having nothing to do with this constantly changing world of becoming and ceasing to be.

2. The individual Self, too, is indestructible, even if it *appears* to be undergoing all these changes. For the Self death is nothing more than casting off a garment. A new one will replace the old one.

3. Even if one doubts the permanence of this Self and believes that birth and death are "real" events, one can see continuity in this continual process of death and renewal, this eternal flux of becoming, passing away, and being reborn.

However comforting all these arguments may sound to the ear of someone facing death, they do seem questionable when we think of the actual human person in real and concrete terms. Life and death are supposed to be hardly more than a costume ball, a drama—so why should Arjuna not plunge right into the thick of battle and fight for his just cause? After all, his real Self cannot be killed there, nor will he be slaying any enemy's Atman. He will only be "taking care" of the Atman's surrounding "sheath," which in the realm of space and time has unfortunately been used in the service of the wrong cause and might therefore be gotten rid of just as well. Indeed, Krishna later comforts Arjuna with the further assurance that He, the cosmic Lord, defeated the enemy long ago, that Arjuna is only performing the deed on the stage of history in the dimension of space and time as an instrument of God, to whom it is also proper to dedicate the fruits of his action.

What is really at issue here is the larger question of the "depersonalization" of the individual. It is through the impersonal view of man that Krishna is trying to solve Arjuna's problem, and this in turn becomes a problem for *us*. So long as the seers of the Upanishads recite the Atman teaching (as it relates to our true nature) in the forest, so to speak, it has for us something inspiring, even fascinating, about it. But when this teaching is transferred to the battle-field, it becomes a little spooky. Yet one could also well ask: is it not precisely here amidst all the killing where this teaching proves its worth? Do we not feel comforted by the certainty that our true Self never dies? Are we not able through this teaching to make some sort of sense of all this "senselessness" precisely because it so clearly points to what remains forever untouched by all these battles, what constitutes its own "sense," so to speak? We stand in admiration before the sage who, anchored unshakably in the eternal Self, even when persecuted and about to be slain, sees the eternal Brahman not only in himself but in his enemy as well. We admire the martyr who regards the torments of the body as nothing, who knows that there is something within him which cannot be touched by his tormentors.

But what about the causal relationship between the doctrine of the Atman and the exhortation to fight? If the destruction of the physical sheath, the body, is really a matter of indifference, then to do battle—then in fact everything—becomes a matter of indifference. Who, then, is Arjuna doing battle with? With ghosts? With empty sheaths? If one does not take death seriously (here in particular the death of another), does life not become ultimately meaningless? Would it then not be merely an empty performance involving non-persons, a puppet show where love is totally absent? Love is possible only between real persons. Can I attack someone with the intention of killing him if I love him? Hardly, it seems—if we don't count acts committed in the heat of passion for reasons of jealousy and the like, acts which really make a caricature of love anyway.

The more I see a living *person* in someone else, a full-fledged human being, someone unique and wonderful, the more impossible it will be for me to destroy this life. What makes killing possible is red-hot hatred, or indifference. The Gita is concerned with the latter. Man becomes a bundle of dispositions and compulsions. He is being divided into an indestructible Atman which has very little to do with this world, and a superficial personality which is all the more caught up in the worldly play of maya, a world where he is dangling blindly by the "strands" of material Nature. Between these two extremes we actually look in vain for the real and responsible human person. "The Lord dwells in the heart of all beings, O Arjuna, and by His maya causes them to revolve as though mounted on a machine," says Krishna in the Gita. (XVIII. 61) Without even intending to be malicious, this may conjure up in people's minds the picture of a dictator stuffing his subjects into uniforms and having them perform a grand opera—or just a Punch-and-Judy show, as the case may be.

As disturbing as these reflections may be to those who have an altogether unquestioning attitude toward the Gita and the Vedantic view of things in general, they are necessary for those who are suffering under the impersonal nature of modern life where the individual no longer counts, where wars and mass annihilation become unreal for the average citizen because he can watch them daily on his television screen, his "maya-box." Today every schoolboy arrives at the conclusion that life is really just a movie. He knows that what he sees in the movies or on television is no real killing, however much he wants it to look real and true to life.

There is no question that the Atman teaching also points in a very positive sense to what is noble in man, to his innately divine nature. It reminds him never to forget that he is the "son of a king." Yet the path to the realization of the Atman must also not bypass what is human in man lest it lead to cruel indifference and inhumanity, instead of a transcendency filled with divine light. Before we experience the invulnerability of the Atman we have to learn to be vulnerable and sensitive, we have to break out of the armor surrounding us. Anyone who has never been deeply affected by something should not take pride in his equanimity. Before we transcend mourning we must be capable of mourning and this we can only do as long as we take people seriously as individuals and act responsibly.

Rather than hindering this sensitivity, the Atman teaching should bring us closer to it, compelling us, as it does, to identify with *all* beings. When Ramakrishna once had to look on when a man was being beaten, the first thing he saw was not the man's invulnerable Atman but his quite real wounds. He recoiled in pain, and on his back appeared the marks of the whip as though he himself had been beaten.

One can use the Atman teaching to justify war, as happens in the Gita, but one can also use it to reject war. I can say: I am not really killing anyone since the true Self of all beings is indestructible, and there is thus no one to be mourned. But once I have experienced the insight that ultimately all beings are part of the indivisible Atman and thus one with myself, I can also say: how could I possibly hurt even the least of beings?

Several passages in the Gita are suggestive of this higher truth. But Krishna seems to be of the opinion that Arjuna, who is still in the midst of life and a member of the warrior caste, should first carve his way through to that truth, even if negatively by the sword, however paradoxical this may sound. Oddly enough, whether in Hinduism, Christianity, or Zen Buddhism, we find besides the ideal of the peaceable sages and saints—who prefer to let themselves be killed rather than do the slightest harm to another sentient being—the ideal of the brave knight or samurai who fears neither death nor the devil and while doing battle with the sword attains states of extreme alertness, indeed at times enlightenment itself. "There are, O best of men, only two men who go beyond the disc of the sun [and reach the realm of Brahma]: the one is the sannyasin immersed in yoga and the other is the warrior falling on the field of battle," says a passage of the Mahabharata. (Udyogaparvan, 32, 65) In order to reach the absolute the yogi (especially the jnana-yogi who takes the Path of Knowledge) must first "eliminate" everything transitory with the so-called Sword of Discrimination. *Neti, neti* is his formidable weapon. Such profound and radical analyzing is thus likened to the feats of a warrior.

All this eliminating should in the end, of course, lead to the knowledge that, fundamentally, there is really nothing to be eliminated. It is at that very point where love would perhaps have a little chance to tentatively raise its head. (For it seems that love is not part of the vocabulary of the sannyasin or the warrior.) When at the end of all this annihilation the illusory nature of this process becomes apparent, when I see even the desire to eliminate as illusion, then a tender "yes" to all there is ought really to emerge. But we must leave the subject here, or rather leave it open, since a more extensive examination of this problem would exceed the compass of this book.

(In *Concordant Discord: The Interdependence of Faiths* [Oxford University Press, 1970], the great book derived from his famous Gifford Lectures, Robert C. Zaehner has already furnished important new ideas on the subject. He

takes into account the overall context of the Mahabharata
and concentrates particularly on the figure of Yudhishtira
who, like Job in the Old Testament, in a way embodies the
"humanistic opposition" to the "awful majesty of God."
Yudhishtira, whose objections to the ethics of the warrior
caste tackle the problem at a much deeper level than Arjuna's somewhat superficial and rather conventional reser-
vations, could rightly be called a forerunner of the peace
movement. In view of the atomic threat and other apocalyptic fears of our era, the time seems in any case more than
ripe for a separate study based on points made in this
Indian epic. Although it would be regrettable, indeed, if
discussions on the problem of war were going to block
access to the wisdom found in the Gita, it would be still
more regrettable if, blinded by the radiance of the divine
guide's authority, one were to forgo certain justified questions of an involved humanism, questions which go far
beyond Arjuna's objections at the beginning of the Gita.)

THE PATH OF CLEAR KNOWLEDGE: JNANA-YOGA

In its teachings the Bhagavad Gita does not confine itself to
one path alone but in accordance with differences in human
make-up offers several possibilities for the realization of
one's divine nature, the Atman. Some of these address the
active type, others the more contemplative type. In addition
to the Path of Knowledge, jnana, prevailing in the Upanishads, we find now also the Path of Loving Devotion
(bhakti) to the divine "friend"; indeed in many verses this
Path of Devotion is even preferred to the Path of Knowledge. Yet despite many a change in emphasis no one path is

played off against another. As the divine source from which all these different paths originate, Krishna remains above the parties. He is like the wishing-tree in the fairy tale to which all wishes are the same; he is the Heavenly Father in whose spacious realm there are many mansions. He does not want to force everyone into the same mold: each is allowed to follow his natural inclination. And he knows when someone lightly chooses a path that is inappropriate to him. Yet, however individually different the paths may be in emphasis and detail—whether they focus more on knowledge of the truth or on loving surrender to a personal God, on meditative mastery over discursive thought or on selfless action—they all have the same aim: the dissolution of the ego and intimate communion, or even union, with the divine.

The teachings of the jnana-path are barely distinguishable from the teachings of the middle and later Upanishads such as the Mundaka, the Katha, and the Svetasvatara Upanishad from which many verses are appropriated directly. We also again find in the Gita the usage of negative terminology in definitions of the nature of the Atman. "This Self is said to be unmanifest, incomprehensible, unchangeable." (II. 25) What is in a sense most self-evident, our true Self, is also what is most enigmatic. Outside the divine ground, that is, in maya—in exile, so to speak—our true state of being seems like something extraordinary, something wondrous. "Some look on the Self as a wonder; some speak of It as a wonder; and some hear of It as a wonder: still others, though hearing, do not understand It at all." (II. 29) And like the rishis of the Upanishads, Krishna uses paradox to describe the Atman-Brahman reality, alternately expressing it negatively, then positively, stressing that the Atman attaches to "no-thing" it permeates and enjoys: "It is without and within all beings. It is unmoving and also moving. It is incomprehensible because it is subtle. It is far away, and yet it is near. . . . It is indivisible, and yet it is, as it were, divided among beings. . . ." (XIII. 15–16) The Atman's omnipresence is illustrated anthropomorphically: "Its hands and feet are everywhere; Its eyes, heads, and faces are everywhere; Its ears are everywhere; Its existence envelops all." (XIII. 13)

Despite repeated emphasis on the ultimate oneness of all that there is, the mental practice of the *jnani* (seeker after knowledge) consists primarily in merciless analyzing, in dividing and separating and making clear distinctions, a process in which the dualism of the Sankhya system is used to special advantage in the Gita. Reality is divided into object and subject, the "field" and the "Knower of the Field." Between these, only a somewhat tenuous relationship seems to exist; sometimes the total absence of any connection between them is stressed. " 'I do nothing at all,' thinks the yogi, the knower of Truth; for in seeing, hearing, touching, smelling, and tasting; in walking, breathing, and sleeping; . . . in speaking, emitting, and seizing; in opening and closing the eyes, he is assured that it is only the senses busied with their objects." (V. 8–9) The Self, the "Knower of the Field," is but the witness, the uninvolved onlooker; the activities of prakriti (primordial Nature), the constant dance of its *gunas* (natural qualities of Nature), are actually of no concern to the Self.

The gunas are the "strands" of Nature which bind man, as we sometimes hear. We should realize, however, that this way of putting it is somewhat misleading since, in a way, sentient beings are altogether made up of these strands; only their inmost nature, the Atman or purusha, is completely free. The three gunas are the *tamas* (darkness, dullness, inertia), *rajas* (ego-driven activity) and—bridging all pairs of opposites—*sattva* (the clear light of harmony and wisdom). The aim of spiritual discipline here is first to overcome inertia (tamas) by activity (rajas)—in which connection *karma-yoga* (which we will be examining later in greater detail) in turn helps in making this activity more and more selfless. In the sattva-guna the light of the Atman is beginning to become visible. At this stage we are "purer" and, having purged ourselves of the grosser forms of ignorance and egotistically purposeful striving, we take pleasure in harmony, wisdom, and beauty. Yet precisely because this guna approaches perfection, there is also a certain danger: we tend to become attached to what is (merely) beautiful and harmonious, we become preoccupied with esthetics, clinging to certain worldly ideals of beauty and harmony. "Of these, sattva, being stainless, is luminous and healthful. It binds, O sinless Arjuna, by creating attachment to happiness and attachment to knowledge." (XIV. 6) Even someone clinging to the blissfulness of religious ecstasy is at bottom still a victim of these gunas because the "field" of prakriti not only encompasses the blind impulses of Nature, but also the world of the mind, including its higher intuitions, manas. As we already indicated, all stirrings of the mind are, in the Sankhya teaching, nothing but the radiance of all-encompassing consciousness mirrored in prakriti (the reflecting mirror of the sattva-guna being much more light-sensitive than that of the rather dull rajas or tamas); and it is this reflection of purusha (pure consciousness) in Nature which makes Nature itself appear intelligent. In the Sankhya teaching, therefore, prakriti resembles a gigantic piece of machinery; even the brightest reflections in the sattva-guna cannot blind us to the mechanical nature of all events, even mental ones. The sage remains as much as possible detached from this sense-less dance of the gunas, alternating as they do between fighting and balancing one another. Of course, he cannot keep from moving and acting altogether as long as he lives in this world of appearances, yet whatever activity is neces-sary for him to keep alive becomes more and more auto-matic. He is aware that all this takes place without him. He does not identify with these activities.

This sage has many traits in common with the stoic who is not ruffled by anything. In the second chapter of the Gita, Arjuna asks Krishna: "What, O Kesava, is the description of a man of steady wisdom merged in samadhi? How does a man of steady wisdom speak, how does he sit, how move?" And Krishna answers: "O Partha, when a man completely casts off all desires of the mind, his Self finding satisfaction in Itself alone, then he is called a man of steady wisdom." (II. 54–55) Someone with such insight is unperturbed by suffering, nor on the other hand clings to pleasure: he has overcome all passions. "He who is not attached to any-thing, who neither rejoices nor is vexed when he obtains good or evil—his wisdom is firmly fixed." (II. 57) There seems to be a coolness, indeed something almost inhuman, about this teaching. But those who feel profound aversion for this kind of joylessness and long for a little warmth and human feeling, however imperfect, in these passionless wastes, ought not close the book too soon. We should bear in mind that the stoic trait represents only one side of the Gita, that it is well balanced by deep love of a personal god and an often very colorfully unfolding pan-en-theism (God-in-all).

Clearly, also, no religion can manage without a certain underlying stoic attitude. The Christian mystics and as-cetics often speak a language very similar to the Gita's.

Toward the end of her life even so passionate a saint as Teresa of Avila came to look on equanimity as the highest virtue. Let us also not forget that mysticism proceeds by dialectical leaps and that it is futile to look in it for an absolute *yes* or *no*. Ultimately, rejection of the world of appearances and total acceptance of it are often very close together. The mystic cannot really accept any reality *apart* from God; but when he is still at a stage where he sees this world as something separate from God he cannot but regard it as little more than "a mound of ashes." Yet once he has arrived at the dimension of the divine he is able again to see the divine in all of Creation. There are numerous passages in the Gita that magnificently proclaim God's immanence in Creation.

We often think of ourselves as saying *yes* to all of Creation and turn away from any religious literature that preaches detachment and renunciation. But is our *yes* really a total *yes*? Does it include all opposites, the whole spread of life—or perhaps only the part that is pleasant and attractive to us? Is it not necessary for total acceptance to be preceded by the practice of nonattachment and equanimity? As long as we are not firmly anchored in the Atman, all we really do is *react*—then call this free and spontaneous action. Without noticing it we are dangling on the strings of prakriti, now pulled this way, now that. This is why the Gita calls passion and hate "the two dangerous enemies on the road" whose power we should not underestimate. (III. 34) The sense organs are tuned by Nature to react positively to certain sense objects or stimulants and negatively to others. As long as the sight, or even the thought of certain things makes us desirous of them, as long as we fly to them—or for that matter flee from them—we are not free. In order to escape this bondage, we can systematically practice saying *yes* to *all* things, even to what appears ugly or terrible (as is done in Tantric practices, for instance). Vedanta begins with the negative path, the path of asceticism: one consciously reins in feelings of attraction and aversion in order to free oneself step by step from the world of the senses, thereby enabling one to become completely absorbed in the dimension of the divine.

Of course, Krishna also knows that this is easier said than done. He knows human nature exceedingly well. Fortunately Arjuna, whom he addresses here, is not the perfect saint but humanness personified. It is therefore easy to identify with him. A purely negative attitude will never lead him, or most of us, to the knowledge of the truth that makes us free, which is why turning *away* from sense objects must be accompanied by a more positive turning *toward* the divine. "The objects of the senses fall away from a man practicing abstinence, but not the taste for them. But even the taste falls away when the Supreme is seen." (II. 59) Since no one can live in a no-man's-land for long, it is close to impossible to become thoroughly detached from the things of this world and our deep-seated passions about them without this positive contemplation of the divine. As long as we have not yet realized this dimension, the sensual aspects of life and our own strong feelings are the positive things that warm us and keep us alive. Anyone who simply turns his back on these things and pursues an entirely negative asceticism runs the risk of losing all vigor and sensitivity. He lives neither in this world nor the other. A living testimony to a worldview conceived in purely negative terms, he wastes away.

Krishna, although employing the negative imagery of Sankhya yoga ("When he completely withdraws the senses from their objects, as a tortoise draws in its limbs, then his wisdom is firmly fixed." [II. 58]), gives this negative type of yoga a strongly theistic positive coloring: "The yogi restrains them [the senses] all and remains intent on Me." (II. 61) Without a firm foundation nothing can be firmly established. In the Gita this foundation is the divine—both the supra-personal Brahman-Atman reality, the divine ground, and the personal creator-god who is incarnate here as Krishna.

One should really not look at any one of the many philosophical and spiritual disciplines in the Gita in isolation but see each within the context of the whole. There is no doubt that what ties them all together is a theistic pan-en-theism: the teaching that everything is God and God is in everything. The Gita avails itself of the Sankhya doctrine when dividing prakriti into its constituents. It then appears to be teaching a distinct dualism. However, just as the original Brahman of the older Upanishads transcends the opposites of purusha/prakriti and really encompasses them both, so in the Gita, Krishna (as Purushottama, XV. 18) encompasses and transcends both the doings of Nature (prakriti) and the unmoving spirit or consciousness (purusha) behind it. He says of himself: "As I surpass the Perishable and as I am higher even than the Imperishable, I am extolled in the world and in the Vedas as the Supreme Self." (XV. 18) We could say that the Brahman of the early Upanishads still encompassed almost unconsciously all the pairs of opposites, including them all within itself. This is the condition *before* all division—even then implying something eternal and beyond. Krishna, on the other hand, stands for the consciously articulated oneness *after* these divisions (associated mostly with Sankhya thought). In his role as avatar (divine incarnation) Krishna combines within himself all seeming opposites: the temporal *and* the eternal, Nature *and* Spirit.

A yogi wanting to free himself from the snares of Nature must first understand all its workings. This illusionless look at Nature which the Sankhya philosophy teaches, far from signaling misguided human thinking, is in fact an important preliminary stage. Such investigating of Nature must, of course, not become an end in itself, or be used for the exclusive purpose of dominating it, as is the tendency in the West. All dualism must eventually be laid to rest again in the superior insight that prakriti is "God's" nature; that although he surpasses it by virtue of his transcendence, he is indeed manifest in all things. This theistic coloring is not only noticeable in the Gita in connection with specific references to *bhakti-yoga,* the Path of Devotion, of loving surrender to the personal god, but also in connection with other yoga paths, whether it be *jnana-, raja-,* or *karma-yoga.* Interestingly, it is in the fourth chapter of the Gita, the one devoted specifically to jnana-yoga, the Path of Knowledge, where Krishna introduced himself as the incarnation of the divine: "For the protection of the good and the destruction of the wicked . . . I am born in every age." (IV. 8) Thus knowledge of the personal god and his involvement in the world—not only the realization of the timeless Atman—is even part of jnana-yoga. However, the Gita (sometimes also referred to as an Upanishad) would not be counted among the Vedantic scriptures if it did not also inject the *bhakta* (worshiper of the personal god)—now ardently adoring this God-incarnation—with a good portion of timeless jnana. To Krishna, what matters is not the physical manifestation itself but that the believer see through this physical manifestation, this veil of maya, and recognize in it—in what seems like a limited historical phenomenon—the eternal formless Lord of the Universe.

THE PATH OF SELFLESS ACTION: KARMA-YOGA

The importance of the theistic element is particularly evident where karma-yoga, the Path of Selfless Action, is taught. In the Vedas the word *karma* (work, deed, or action, and its resulting effect) referred mainly to the performance of works in the sense of ritual offerings and sacrifice. In the Bhagavad Gita, too, sacrifice plays a significant role—indeed all Creation is regarded as a single great offering. But when teaching Arjuna the path of karma-yoga, Krishna does not so much have in mind sacrificial offerings in the context of a religious cult, as any work or action, however ordinary and insignificant, selflessly performed. Sri Aurobindo's motto, "All of life is yoga," could have been lifted from the Gita.

With his high praise of the ascetic path, or jnana-yoga, his exhortation to free himself from the things of this world, Krishna appears to have confused Arjuna, because he no longer knows now whether to act or not to act. That is why Krishna says to him: "Not by merely abstaining from action does a man reach the state of actionlessness, nor by mere renunciation does he arrive at perfection." (III. 4) Krishna also calls a hypocrite someone who has outwardly withdrawn from the world (doing "the yogi-thing," as it were), "but continues to dwell in his mind on the objects of his senses." (III. 6) He much prefers one who outwardly still lives in the midst of life and "does his al-

lotted action"—but without attachment and clinging to
things.

It is not easy to characterize this ideal of Indian karma-
yoga. It lies somewhere between the Taoist *wu-wei,* allowing things their way, and the Prussian adherence to duty.
Unlikely as this sounds, it resembles a combination of Lao-
tzu and Kant—with a peacock feather, symbol of Krishna,
the ornament connecting them. The Prussian element can
sometimes be a little disturbing; but again, only if one
isolates it from the rest. There is much talk of obedience
and duty. It is also understood that even when one per-
forms one's duty with all one's might, the *fruits* of one's
actions are not one's own to enjoy. (Particularly these days,
when the old work ethic is beginning to show cracks everywhere, this yoga path is not likely to find many enthusiasts
if it is presented merely as a dry concept of duty.) Why,
some may ask, should Arjuna do his duty at all, especially
the duty of a soldier, when everything is meaningless anyway? Does this not amount to something like the labor of
Sisyphus—an activity in a climate of absurdity?

The universe Krishna describes in the Gita has no purpose, after all; indeed Krishna himself admits that he has no
real motive; that the acts both of creating (or projecting-out-
of-himself) and of preserving are not things he *needs* to do:
"I have, O Partha, no duty; there is nothing in the three
worlds that I have not gained and nothing that I have to gain.
Yet I continue to work." (III. 22) We, who are still pursuing
goals and look for meaning in everything, may ask *why?*
Krishna's subsequent declaration that he acts in order to set
a good example for mankind does not really satisfy us. "For
should I not ever engage, unwearied, in action, O Patha,
men would in every way follow in my wake. . . . If I should
cease to work, these worlds would perish: I should cause

confusion and the destruction of all creatures." (III. 23–24) *So,* we ask, if no real motive for Creation exists, then why should it matter whether the whole thing collapses or not?

It is obvious why the question of *meaning* comes up again and again in connection with the Gita. If the world is indeed nothing but a gigantic piece of machinery, why should it be kept going at all costs? A Westerner with a Calvinistic-capitalist background can at least hold on to the performance principle: I have accomplished something, I have created something—even if his faith prohibits him from enjoying the fruits of his labor too much. Accomplishment here equals meaningfulness. Yet in the Gita man is robbed even of this kind of satisfaction. It seems he may act only for the sake of action. Despite its soberness, Kant's famous Categorical Imperative is still addressed to a world where performance "counts," where labor has a "value." But the moment this concept of duty becomes part of a worldview where the universe is conceived of as little more than a puppet theater—with marionettes dancing on strings—it becomes pretty spooky again. In the end one may ask: Is there really any difference between pure motiveless activity and just sheer *being*—and how does that differ from *nonbeing*? And whether or not we are aware of it, this question brings us very close to the heart of the matter.

God creates "without a why," said Meister Eckhart, and according to him the righteous man also lives without asking *why.* Why-questions arise in maya, in the realm of space, time and causality. They arise when we think in categories of beginning and end, performance and profit, motive and goal, etc. Someone enlightened is no longer in need of a motive; and God—who we may assume is enlightened—needs no motive for his works either. That is one reason why he sometimes offers somewhat lame explanations to those still needing explanations. Then he plays Immanuel Kant (with a barely suppressed chuckle). On his own he practices wu-wei, the art of actionless action—which nevertheless brings everything about. "Tao never does, but through it, all is done," says Lao-tzu. (18) And Krishna declares: "He who sees inaction in action, and action in inaction, he is wise among men . . . giving up attachment to the fruit of action and dependent on none, though engaged in work, he (the sage) does no work at all." (IV. 18, 20)

Most people achieve this maturity and wisdom only toward the end of a long life of ego-driven activity, perhaps only after many lives; but God's wisdom is not the end result of anything, but beginningless beginning itself. His has been non-attachment all along; he has no needs, not even the need to create. It is from this utter *freedom* that creation and renewal continue to flow as his offering. The Universal Lord of the Gita is no Hegelian absolute and does not depend on history for its realization. For him creating is overabundance, play. He is agent and onlooker all at once, he is both within and without all things. Those who do not yet understand identify too much with their actions.

Elsewhere Krishna stresses that the wise should not "unsettle the understanding of the ignorant who are still attached to action. He should engage them in action, himself performing it with devotion." (III. 26) In this connection even the Categorical Imperative takes on a new meaning; because, if the ignorant did not follow a good example, they would only sink to the level of tamas, into darkness, dullness, and indolence—thus never attaining to superior actionless action.

According to the Gita, Creation has been under way from all eternity as the spontaneous outpouring of the Lord's creative energy, as the workings of his prakriti (primordial Nature). Yet all this spontaneity and freedom, so natural to God, has yet to be discovered and realized by the numberless creatures involved in this process. (It is as if Creation were playing hide-and-seek with itself.) Thus it is important to be accepting of each sentient being and deal with it in accordance with its own nature and level of development. There are some people, for instance, who are at a level of understanding where the idea of absolute freedom—something not allowing for a *why*—simply does not make sense, is absurd, and spells chaos. Advocating spontaneity here would merely lead to license; advocating actionless action merely to laziness; and detachment from things—far from giving rise to transcendental joyfulness— would lead only to blind cynicism.

This is why Krishna urges taking all one does seriously— regardless of the overall playfulness. ("Yoga is skill in action." [II. 50.]) The path is at least as important as the goal—indeed, one should be "casting off attachment and remain even-minded both in success and failure." (II. 48) Not to be confused with merely not caring, this even- mindedness is good advice. It is an aid in becoming so absorbed in the process that the goal fades from memory, no longer something we cling to. Constantly having an eye on the payoff really leads only to tension. It is better to do what we have to do without being tense, a condition also allowing for greater alertness.

THE PATH OF LOVING DEVOTION: BHAKTI-YOGA

Without the bhakti element, however—without the love of God suffusing karma-yoga with a little warmth—karma-yoga would seem to have something mechanical about it. This is not to say that it could not be practiced by itself, only that love, here as elsewhere, considerably facilitates things because the person lovingly devoted to God is automatically above questions of "meaning." Everything he does he does for the sake of Him, the Lord (or for the sake of Her, the Divine Mother). Why? Because it makes him happy. And why does it make him happy? Because it fills him with love. One could continue this into infinity. There is no better evidence that love is one with true being than that it takes one beyond causality, beyond *why* questions. (Which is unfortunately also the reason why it is open to abuse.)

Because in spiritual love all works are an offering to God, bhakti-yoga also quite naturally concerns itself more with karma-speculations. This kind of devotion plays a major role throughout the Gita. Through it the devotee not only renounces all claim to the fruits of his deeds—and thereby is free from pride and conceit—but also does not get caught up in feelings of guilt when something goes awry. His reasoning is that since God supports this entire universe, he will bear his small burden as well. He thus leaves all else to God; he does his best—that's all.

Despite this kind of intimacy the bhakti-path of the Gita is still relatively tempered compared with the passionate enthusiasm exhibited by later bhakti-cults that center around the Lord Krishna. The Krishna in the Gita, just like the Buddha, teaches the Middle Way. He warns against excesses such as extremes in asceticism. One may wonder whether *this* Krishna would have been very comfortable with the erotic hothouse atmosphere of many a later Krishna cult.

The Gita nevertheless represents a great step forward when it comes to both simplifying and intensifying man's relationship with the divine. Krishna does not ask his believers for elaborate sacrificial rituals: "Whoever offers Me, with devotion, a leaf, a flower, a fruit, or water—that I accept, the pious offering of the pure in heart. Whatever you do, whatever you eat, whatever you offer in sacrifice, whatever you give away, and whatever you practice in the way of austerities, O son of Kunti—do it as an offering to Me." (IX. 26–27) Thus in the end, through daily devotion, all existence becomes one joyful offering to God. Here at last jnana-, bhakti-, karma-, and raja-yoga all combine to become a single flame of knowledge, love, works, and meditation.

Krishna also loves the jnani (follower of the Path of Knowledge) who becomes absorbed in the impersonal absolute, but he draws attention to the fact that this path is more difficult. (XII. 5) Because of the great difficulty of freeing himself from the passions, man finds it easier to redirect his natural emotions toward the personal god. With love as a lubricant everything is easier and concentration on the object of love is not something he has to force; it happens of itself. The great advantage of the bhakti-path is that it is natural. It also lends something of this naturalness and spontaneity to the other yoga-paths when it influences them.

Anyone taking up the Gita and studying it intensely should be especially intent on trying to uncover the *real* substance of this work. This is all the more important since today's Western reader, unlike his Indian counterpart, is not able to approach the Gita with reverence alone and accept it as though it were the eternal repository of truth, somehow decreed from on high. Many a prejudice of the time has gotten mixed up in it that we need not forthwith adopt, things like the caste system, the position of women, or the meaning of war. A few other timeless problems also remain on the table no matter how sympathetic the interpretation, such as questions concerning the dignity and reality of the individual and those concerning the reason for all the goings-on in the universe and what it all "means." Anyone, for instance, who shares the dynamic worldview of a Sri Aurobindo or a Teilhard de Chardin will probably not be completely satisfied with what, ultimately, amounts to a static worldview, no matter how much he likes the Gita. Although there are occasionally small signs of a more historical and evolutionary conception of the universe—for instance, the intervention of the *avatar* in the affairs of the world—it nevertheless remains a closed universe where nothing ever really changes. However much Krishna exhorts man to action, he never seems to contemplate a joyfully creative transformation of this world. Looked at through the eyes of the Gita, the world of prakriti is actually a rather sad state of affairs, a vale of tears from which one ought to free oneself as quickly as possible in order to reach one's heavenly home, the Lord. There is thus little difference between the worldviews of the Gita, Buddhism, and the medieval Imitation of Christ.

We should also, of course, consider this: if we take the liberty of calling into question sacred texts such as the Bhagavad Gita here and there, then we ought also to allow such a scripture to question *us*—along with our ego-bound shortsightedness. Thus any verse we find hard to swallow *as is* might, for instance, have the positive side effect of throwing some light on this or that weakness in *ourselves*. What is important at all times are not philosophical arguments as to whether or not this or that worldview is the correct one, but that through intensive study of such texts we spiritually grow. A scriptural text is like a guru we see every day. Perhaps one thing or another about him does not suit us, but we would profit little from this daily contact if we were unable to get beyond our objections, if we did not also tussle with him in a more positive sense—and at other times empty ourselves of our own ideas to simply let the substance do its work.

There certainly is enough of this in the Gita to nourish and sustain us for a lifetime. This substance has always had something sacramental about it, which is why it cannot be analyzed by purely rational maneuvers. It is something thoroughly positive, almost tangible even, and especially when it remains a mystery to us. This applies particularly to all those passages in the Gita that speak of a cosmic sacrifice and the immanence of the divine in all things. We have the impression we are leaving behind the sphere of philosophical and theological debate here and entering the Mystery itself. "To him Brahman is the offering, and Brahman is the oblation, and it is Brahman who offers the oblation in the fire of Brahman. Brahman alone is attained by him who thus sees Brahman in action." (IV. 24) Especially when such verses are chanted as grace before meals (in the uniquely powerful Sanskrit) something of the sacramental nature of this verse comes across. Here the dualistic split created by Sankhya analysis vanishes and questions of meaning become ultimately meaningless; here we find ourselves in the midst of reality—oneness is suddenly not something abstract and philosophical any longer, but tangible. Such verses are not the product of a top-heavy intellect; they issue from the center, from the heart of the universe and from Him who brought forth this universe.

To such passages also belong those celebrating the immanence of the divine where Krishna presents himself as the essence or vitality of all things: "I am the savour of waters, O son of Kunti, the radiance of the sun and moon; I am the syllable OM in all the Vedas, the sound in ether, the manliness in man. . . . I am the sweet fragrance in earth and the brightness in fire. In all beings I am the life, and I am the austerity in ascetics. Know me, O son of Pritha, to be the Eternal Seed of all things that exist; I am the intelligence of the intelligent and the daring of the brave." (VII. 8–10)

A thin line here separates the pan-en-theism (God-in-all), so typical of the Gita, from crude pantheism. Krishna does not identify wholly with the manifestations of Nature. He often enough points to his radical transcendence: "By Me, in my unmanifested form, are all things in this universe pervaded. All beings exist in Me, but I do not exist in them. . . . And yet the beings do not dwell in Me—behold, that is My divine mystery. My Spirit, which is the support of all beings and the source of all things, does not dwell in them." (IX. 4–5)

Anyone not familiar with mystical dialectics may be at a loss here. For him there are only two alternatives: either God is completely outside Creation or he coincides with it. In the spirit of mysticism, which also rules the Gita, the matter presents itself something like this: it is precisely God's being completely transcendent and independent of all beings and manifestations that makes him appear free to become all things—out of this transcendental void.

Someone approaching God through the world of appearances is at first only able to detect certain degrees of divine manifestation, of course. The mere surface of things is not going to reveal to him the divine right away. He must press on to the heart, or essence of things, just as Shvetaketu did in the Chandogya Upanishad when his father, Uddalaka, urged him on to keep dividing the seed of the banyan tree until nothing was visible any more and his father could say: "That subtle essence, in it all that exists has its self. That is the True. That is the Self. That thou art, Shvetaketu." (VI. xii. 1) Whether we call it Atman or conceive of it as the "Lord who pervades all," we always have to start with the tangible to reach the intangible, proceed from matter to energy, to the creative intelligence driving it. This is a kind of mystical atom-splitting. (It seems hardly surprising that some modern physicists are discovering new doors to metaphysics and mysticism.) One could imagine the apocryphal saying, attributed to Jesus, that in order to find Him, one need only "split the wood and lift the stone," as coming equally well from the mouth of Krishna—who never exhausts himself in the world, who is no extra-cosmic creator-god intervening in history from *without*. Krishna is also a god of Nature, a god of spring who causes everything to unfold and blossom.

In statements of inescapable poetic power Krishna again and again sheds light on his nature, illuminating it from all angles and showing us his universality. "I am the [Vedic] sacrifice, I am the worship, I am the oblation to the dead, and I am the food. I am the hymn, I am the melted butter, I am the fire, and I am the offering. . . . I am the father of the universe, the mother, the sustainer, and the grandsire. I am the knowable, the purifier, and the syllable OM. I am also the Rik, the Saman, and the Yagus [Vedas]. . . . I am the goal and the support; the lord and the witness; the abode, the refuge, and the friend. I am the origin and the dissolution; the ground, the storehouse, and the imperishable seed. . . . I give heat; I hold back and send forth rain. I am immortality, O Arjuna, and also death. I am being and also non-being." (IX. 16–19)

We have already emphasized that nothing is excluded

from this universality, everything is included: "Even those
devotees who, endowed with faith, worship other gods,
worship Me alone, O son of Kunti, though in a wrong
way. . . . For I alone am the Enjoyer and the Lord of all
sacrifice. . . ." (IX. 23–24) Krishna only makes *this* distinction: although anyone worshiping other gods (the Vedic
gods, for example) will for a time partake of the joys of
their particular heavens, he must perforce be born again
and continue to perfect himself when his good karma is
exhausted. But whoever lovingly and wholly surrenders to
Him, the Lord of the universe and origin of all gods, he
attains to that place from where there is no more returning.
The Gita leaves it open as to whether this entering into the
Lord stands for complete absorption in the divine or a
sharing in the celestial glory wherein the soul still retains its
individuality.

In chapter 10 of the Gita we again find Krishna emphasizing his immanence in Creation—this time by referring to
himself as the first and all-highest of a species of beings and
deities, as the perfect archetype, as it were, from which all
the others are derived. He concludes this long list with the
words: "There is no end of My divine manifestations, O
dreaded Arjuna. This is but a partial statement by Me of the
multiplicity of My attributes. . . . Whatever glorious or
beautiful or mighty being exists anywhere, know that it has
sprung from but a spark of My splendor. . . . But what need
is there of your acquiring this detailed knowledge, O Arjuna? With a single fragment of Myself I stand supporting
the whole universe." (X. 40–42)

The knowledge of the *one* is needed, not the knowledge
of the many. Krishna seems to be playing down these numberless manifestations—the mere listing of which so daz-

zled Arjuna—the better to draw attention to his true nature, to the string holding all these bright and shiny pearls together.

THE AWESOME MAJESTY OF GOD

In chapter 11, perhaps the most famous in the Gita, Krishna appears again before Arjuna in his full and this time awe-inspiring majesty. To enable him to behold his far-flung powers he lends Arjuna the Celestial Eye. What follows is a sheer endless profusion of images of the *mysterium tremendum et fascinosum,* causing the amazed and frightened Arjuna's hair to stand on end. "If the radiance of a thousand suns were to burst forth at once in the sky, that would be like the splendor of the Mighty One." (XI. 12) Then Arjuna sees the entire universe being devoured by Krishna's many flaming mouths: all gods, men and other beings, including all those assembled on the battlefield. "You lickest Thy lips, devouring all the worlds on every side with Thy flaming mouths. Thy fiery rays fill the whole universe with their radiance and scorch it, O Vishnu! . . . Tell me who Thou art that wearest this frightful form. Salutations to Thee, who are the Primal One; for I do not understand Thy purpose." (XI. 30–31) To this Krishna replies: "I am mighty world-destroying Time, now engaged here in slaying these men. Even without you, all these warriors standing arrayed in the opposing armies shall not live." (XI. 32) Arjuna, breaking into hymns of praise again, is horrified to think that he has hitherto treated this divine, supra-cosmic figure like any normal human friend, someone to be taken rather lightly. Recognizing in this awesome being the primeval creator and destroyer of all worlds, he implores "Him with a thousand arms and terrible mouths" to return to his old familiar form. In response Krishna takes on his "lovely" form again—so bewitching to mankind— then assures Arjuna that there are few only who, by his grace, ever see him in his cosmic form.

A comparison of this eleventh chapter of the Gita with certain passages in the Upanishads might be useful. Anyone coming from the Upanishads and turning to the Gita will probably be struck at first by the apocalyptic power of this imagery which, in this exact same form, is nowhere to be found in the Upanishads. Yet there are all kinds of precedents and cross-connections.

Thus we read in the Katha Upanishad of prana, the breath of life or cosmic energy: "Whatever there is—the whole universe—vibrates because it has gone forth from Brahman, which exists as its Ground. That Brahman is a great terror, like a poised thunderbolt. Those who know It become immortal. . . . From terror of Brahman, fire burns; from terror of It, the sun shines; from terror of It Indra and Vyahu, and Death, the fifth, run." (II. iii. 1–2)

In a verse in the Svetasvatara Upanishad, Rudra is worshiped as the highest god and entreated not to destroy this world, following an appeal to this *benign* face for protection from his wrathful nature. Those who are fearful pray to him: "O Rudra, do not, in Thy wrath, destroy our children and grandchildren. Do not destroy our lives; do not destroy our cows or horses; do not destroy our servants. For we invoke Thee always." (IV. 22)

Certain "positive" images in the Upanishads become "negative" in the Gita: "As flowing rivers disappear into the sea, losing their names and forms, so a wise man, freed

from name and form, attains the Purusha, who is greater
than the Great," we read in the Mundaka Upanishad. (III.
ii. 8) Then, in the eleventh chapter of the Gita, we find these
verses: "As the many torrents of the rivers rush toward the
ocean, so do the heroes of the mortal world rush into Thy
fiercely flaming mouths. . . . As moths rush swiftly into a
blazing fire, even so do these creatures swiftly rush into
Thy mouths to their own destruction." (XI. 28–29) In
both cases we are dealing with "annihilation," but with a
difference. The Upanishad verse describes how those enlightened, those who have experienced unity with the all-
highest, are absorbed by it like rivers by the sea. In the
corresponding verses of the Gita we are dealing with "devouring," with the veritable pulverization of the universe in
general and the killing of warriors in particular. In a sense
the warriors also disappear into God, are absorbed by him,
not to enter the realm of perfection but to face further death
and chaos in order to be readied for a new birth. The
enlightened ones, now nameless and formless, merge with
the absolute never to return; while these warriors lose their
form temporarily, crushed by Krishna's terrible jaws, to be
reborn again from the womb of all that is subject to becoming and passing away—until in the end they too attain
ultimate liberation in him.

Although the description of God, "with myriad arms
and bellies, with myriad faces and eyes" (XI. 16) also occurs in the Upanishads, one senses the approach of a new
era, a time nearer to what we call popular Hinduism. The
images become more colorful and detailed, on one hand
fiercer, on the other more naive. We are beginning to
touch on the world of the Puranas, the popular myths and
tales. God's majesty is now being depicted more and more
in maya-images that have a powerful emotional effect on

the believer and cause him to prostrate himself. Although belonging to the warrior caste, Arjuna is not made of the same stuff as the intrepid Nachiketa of the Upanishads who was not so easily impressed. Arjuna is a bhakta with palms held together in prayer, the very embodiment of reverence.

While in the Upanishads the realization of the *Atman* was the highest aim, in the Gita it is the vision of the all-sublime deity, the *Bhagavan*, which receives the highest praise. "Neither by the Vedas, nor by penances, nor by alms-giving, nor yet by sacrifice, am I to be seen in the form in which you have now beheld Me," (XI. 53) says Krishna, using almost the identical words the Katha and Mundaka Upanishads used when speaking of the realization of the Atman.

Although an element of grace is implied even in the Upanishads—since it is expressly stated that the realization of the Atman cannot be the result of human effort—the central focus is the Atman, the invisible, formless Self indwelling in all beings, even gods, and not the multifarious and colorful forms of a personal god before whom men fall prostrate to the ground.

We may recall the Isha Upanishad where the seer asks the Lord to gather his rays, to withdraw his light so he "would see, through His grace" that "I am indeed He that Purusha, who dwells there." (16) The very glare and splendor of omnipotence is what obscures the innermost truth: the actual not-two-ness of God and man. From the standpoint of *Advaita* Vedanta all the "splendor" Krishna displays in chapter 11 and verses leading up to it belongs, ultimately, also to the Atman of every human being; it is only that Krishna, by his *yoga-maya*, has the power to make visible the greatness of the Atman. One might say that he is a kind of celestial movie projectionist. The extent to which one is impressed by this apocalyptical display rests, of course, with each individual alone.

Arjuna's pleading with Krishna to reveal himself in his more familiar and humanlike form, after so dazzling him with his terrifying majesty, is not unlike this passage in the Isha Upanishad. Where realization of the Atman and unity with the divine begin to recede into the background and the figure of Ishvara, the personal God, is clearly becoming more prominent, a chasm between God and man—one we know only too well from the Semitic revelatory religions—threatens to open up. It is to bridge this chasm that God must incarnate in human form. Arjuna's longing for Krishna to return to his original familiar form, after revealing to him his awesome divine powers, really conceals the unconscious desire for the confirming insight that this original form has indeed something to do with the "little man," the "thumb-sized" purusha, dwelling in the hearts of all men, which plays such an important role in the Upanishads. Nothing outshines the Atman—which is both smaller than the smallest and greater than the greatest—not even the imposing (movie) projections of the divine maya as found in the eleventh chapter of the Gita.

We are entering here the peculiar zone in Vedanta, between bhakti and jnana, where the polemical sparks fly as to the relative merits of each, and where a Vedantin must decide whether he belongs to the party of Shankara and his Advaita Vedanta or shares more the worldview and vision of a personal god prevailing in the later bhakti schools. (We shall be dealing with these two schools of thought in greater detail in the next chapters.)

For some people the Gita's theism represents a step backward, for others a clear step forward. I would consider it at least an enrichment. It does not represent a break with the Upanishads, the truths of which shine through strongly enough; indeed the Gita has made many of these truths popular with some believers who would otherwise perhaps never have been interested in the Upanishads. While the Atman teaching forms only part of the great edifice that is the Gita, its essential features are indeed preserved there.

Also, in chapter 15 of the Gita, Krishna speaks of two principles in the world: the "perishable" and the "imperishable." To himself he refers as the All-Supreme or *Purushottama* who encompasses and transcends both the perishable (comprising all creatures), and the imperishable (or unchanging principle within them). Sri Aurobindo compared this god to a bird whose two wings represent these two principles, the dynamic and the static. Whatever one's view on the matter, it is and remains an important effort of the Indian mind to transcend the onesidedness of Sankhya dualism as well as the onesidedness of some currents in Vedanta which overstress the impersonal. There is little doubt that, generally, theism does more to shape the belief of most Hindus than does Shankara's pure Advaita— where the personal god is allowed only a relatively shadowy existence "beneath" the attributeless Brahman. But more of this in the next chapter.

Advaita: The Philosophy of Non-Duality

Of the two philosophical concepts *dvaita* and *a-dvaita* (from the Sanskrit roots for *two* and *not-two*) or duality and non-duality respectively, advaita stands for the ultimate *oneness* of reality, the main concern of the Advaita school of Vedanta.

When first coming across texts dealing with pure Advaita teaching—such as, for instance, the Ashtavakra Samhita or Gaudapada's *Karika*, a commentary on the Mandukya Upanishad—one tends to have one of two possible reactions: either one considers them the writings of men who have been out in the blazing sun for too long, or one likens them to the sun itself in its power to dispel darkness, convinced that they are *the* answer and solution to all questions and problems, that they constitute the human mind's last breakthrough to absolute truth. The radical nature of these texts does not really allow for a position somewhere in between these two extremes, certainly not a lukewarm and patronizing "very interesting." The challenge to our accustomed views is so dramatic and unsettling that it comes down to either a perception of total nonsense or highest wisdom.

We normally expect philosophy to furnish answers to our questions in a more or less orderly fashion, to deal with our problems in great detail, and to enlighten us as to the meaning of life; in other words to *explain* things to us. But in Advaita Vedanta nothing at all is explained; instead, everything is explained away. This is so because Advaita does not so much concern itself with the questions being asked as with what causes them to arise in the first place: man's ego. Then we are told that this ego is something altogether unreal, as unreal as the illusory universe. The teachers of Advaita Vedanta keep telling us that if we "apply the axe to the root of the *I*," the whole illusory world will vanish—along with all its perplexing diversity—and in a flash reality, or Brahman, the one-without-a-second, will be seen.

Even if one can call the Advaita teaching a philosophy—as we have done in the chapter title—it is in no way the intention of its teachers to construct yet another philosophical system. If anything, they wish to reduce this kind of activity. With a sharp eye for such things, they are thus content to merely point to the many contradictions in which the dualistic schools are entangled—then, with a kindly smile, take up residence, so to speak, in the apparent emptiness of non-duality. The Advaitin, stresses Gaudapada (a precursor of Shankara), does not quarrel with anyone. He sees the relative value of provisional truth. While the religious and philosophical hotheads debate the godhead and the individual soul, and so forth, the Advaitin is much too far removed from such concerns to get excited over these things. Concepts of how the one relates to the other, and all the problems connected with such ideas, can exist only where there is still a perception of not *one*, but *two*. The Advaitin lives in the *one*, sees only the *one*, or more precisely: that which is *not-two*. (Because it is still possible to become attached to "the one" and make of it an ideology—such as a rigid monism—thereby creating yet another philosophical system.) Because of the dualistic nature of words, the true Vedantin prefers not to get involved in debate. He is like the old music teacher in Hermann Hesse's *Glass Bead Game* who just keeps smiling at the constantly questioning Josef Knecht, then finally says to him, "You're tiring yourself out, Josef. . . ."

THE GREAT SHANKARA

Despite what has been said so far, not even Advaita was spared the inevitable descent into polemical disputes. In fact, its most famous representative, Shankaracharya ("Shankara the Teacher," or "Shankara" for short), often celebrated as the prince of Vedanta philosophy, was also a brilliant dialectician and debater. (We are reminded of the High Middle Ages in Europe when, during the course of the disputes between Franciscans and Dominicans, even an "Advaitin" like Meister Eckhart—who should have been above the fray—was sent to the front lines, to Paris.) India did not always reserve its highest esteem for the silent mystic alone, but also admired the eloquent debater and his ability to combine mystical insight with penetrating philosophical reasoning, even at times driving his opponents to burn themselves to death after losing the battle of words. Shankara is said to have thus driven numerous Buddhists to suicide. Even if there is no real connection between these fires and the burnings at the stake during our Inquisition, these incidents nevertheless show that things could get pretty hot in so-called tolerant India as well.

Shankara lived around A.D. 800 and, according to legend, died at the age of thirty-two. A precocious youth, he composed a great many important writings in his short life. Although not considered an avatar in the traditional sense, like Rama or Krishna, he is regarded as an *acharya,* a religious authority; yet many of his most ardent admirers consider him an embodiment of Shiva, the eternal guru, the jnani par excellence. He was born into a Brahmin family on the Malabar Coast and thus, like all great acharyas, came from the south of India. Among the writings attributed to him are the commentaries on the Brahma Sutras, commentaries on the chief Upanishads and the Bhagavad Gita, as well as the shorter didactic poems such as the Vivekacudamani and the Atmabodha; indeed even some of the most beautiful bhakti-hymns in praise of the personal god are said to derive from the pen of this great jnani.

When Shankara was born, Buddhism was already in sharp decline in India and many Hindus proudly claim that Shankara himself did a great deal to finally drive it out of India altogether. He strengthened orthodoxy by encouraging people to return to the study of the Vedas. Traveling the length and breadth of India he preached his doctrine and founded an important order of Hindu monks whose monasteries continue to be strongholds of Advaita Vedanta to this day and who enjoy great authority among the people. Shankara restored confidence among Hindus in their religion by presenting them (and the rest of the world) with an imposing spiritual edifice which accommodated practically everyone's belief: at the everyday level the popular belief in many deities; above this, the belief in the *one* Ishvara, creator, preserver, and destroyer of the universe; and above *this,* Ishvara transcended by the knowledge of the absolute, supra-personal Brahman—which, through maya, appears on the relative plane as the personal god and the world of multiple phenomena.

Shankara so forcefully stressed that *Nirguna* Brahman is absolute and *without* attributes, however, that by this alone the lower levels, along with the creator-god, seemed eclipsed and their independent reality seriously called into question. Nirguna literally means "without gunas," that is without the qualities found in prakriti or Nature. Included among these would, of course, also be omnipotence, wisdom, compassion, and such other characteristics as are commonly associated with God. Shankara calls the *personal* god—who can of necessity only be thought of in connection with Creation and the gunas of prakriti— *Saguna* Brahman, or Brahman *with* attributes; but accords him validity only on the lower, relative levels of understanding.

All such concepts, along with man's sensation of a separate "I" and the perception of a manifold outer world, vanish in the depth of *nirvikalpa samadhi,* that state of absorption where opposites and distinctions cancel each other out. Because this state is devoid of reference points and there is nothing to compare it to, it is inexpressible. Since no separate "I" can be said to exist in this state, there is, of course, also no "entity" capable of reciting Shankara's verse where he praises this highest state of knowledge: "I am this Brahman, One-without-a-second, taintless, immortal Reality, beyond ideas of I and thou, or this and that, the Essence of Infinite Bliss, the Highest Truth." (Vivekacudamani, 493) These are clearly later rationalizations, attempts by the mystic to translate his experience into the language of metaphysical cliché; yet they still echo the wonder and jubilation of true realization.

One may well have wondered what distinction, if any, was left between this Nirguna Brahman "beyond ideas of I and thou," and the *sunyata*, or "voidness" of Mahayana Buddhism. The irony was that Shankara's techniques of negation placed him in a peculiar light: the fervent opponent of the Buddhist schools came himself to be called a crypto-Buddhist, and it was precisely Shankara's intellectual superstructure—not without a certain Buddhist hue—which, while giving new life to orthodox Hinduism, also in the end caused everyday popular Hindu beliefs to be left behind and mired in unreality.

However aggressively Shankara argued against the Buddhists, he was nevertheless indebted to them for having cleared the air and left behind a climate more conducive to clarity of thought. Both parties learned from each other. Shankara, like his immediate predecessor Gaudapada (his guru's guru), read the Upanishads with the same eyes as Nagarjuna, one of the principal representatives of Mahayana Buddhism. Nagarjuna had distinguished between two levels of reality, one relative, one absolute. This double standard of truth, which was to become so immensely important in Shankara's system of thought (and which in modified form we also find in the Christian sphere, for instance in the Alexandrians Clement and Origen), was nowhere quite so developed in earlier Hindu texts—that is, not counting the one mention in the Mundaka Upanishad where a distinction is hinted at between a higher and a lower knowledge. (I.i.3–4) Indeed, Shankara was accused of having introduced a foreign element into Hinduism with this double-standard approach and thereby having violated the spirit of the sacred scriptures.

However that may be, for Shankara this doctrine was above all a convenient teaching method when dealing with the many difficulties and apparent contradictions in the scriptures. He explained it by saying that the seers of the Upanishads had spoken to two different kinds of people: those still seeking after the truth and for whom the multiplicity of Creation was still real, and those already enlightened and for whom there existed only the one Brahman, the one-without-a-second, devoid of any attributes. Similarly, when it was pointed out to him that the scriptures did attribute qualities to the Brahman and that they also spoke of the universe arising from Brahman, he would say that in such instances the scriptures employed a figurative way of speaking for the benefit of seekers for whom the absolute truth was something too abstract to contemplate and comprehend. The idea that the Brahman literally brings forth Creation, along with individual beings, he said, was only a relative and provisional truth, a way of making the believer see the Brahman as our true origin and eternal home, that in reality there was no such thing as emerging from the Brahman or returning to the Brahman. All these "events," including the ideas of reincarnation—the wandering of the individual soul through countless forms of existence—and God's becoming flesh as the avatar, he said, were mere maya, nothing but maya.

MAYA, THE INDIAN SPHINX

The term *maya* plays a pivotal role in Shankara's philosophical system, so much so that it is often called *Maya-vada* (maya-teaching); and since Shankara's philosophy continued to prevail and was identified with Vedanta (which it still is today), the words *Vedanta* and *maya* came to be inseparably linked in people's minds.

In the Upanishads, the actual basis for Vedanta, the word *maya* occurs hardly at all. Originally it meant something like "magic" or "miraculous power," for example the power by which a deity could cause itself to instantly appear, disappear, or otherwise transform. In the comparatively late Svetasvatara Upanishad, maya is said to be "the [creative] power belonging to the Lord Himself and hidden in its gunas." (I.3) Maya begins to merge with prakriti here. Perceived as separate from the Self, it becomes the eternal *object*. Yet even in later times the word *maya* retained something of its original magic and mysteriousness, while *prakriti* referred more to matter, to the whole matrix of Nature. In the Gita we find both connotations, maya sometimes being the negative principle there, sometimes the positive principle. Negatively conceived, maya is what blinds man and, for instance, prevents Arjuna from realizing that Krishna, although incarnate in human form, is in reality the Lord of the Universe; while positively conceived, maya is the "magic" power that enables Krishna to become incarnate and still reveal himself to Arjuna as the cosmic Lord. The great variety of forms maya takes detracts from the underlying oneness; all these phenomena act like a veil. Just as ever-changing cloud formations conceal the blue sky beyond, so constant mental and physical activity conceals the underlying pure consciousness. But then again, maya is also responsible for Krishna's magnificent display of his many divine manifestations which so impressed Arjuna.

Shankara took all these ideas and developed them into a systematic doctrine in which, it must be admitted, the negative connotation of maya predominates. This is not to say, however, that he forthwith attributed only the negative principle to maya while attributing the positive principle to a "good" Brahman. To this great Vedanta philosopher the entire world of phenomena—from the tiniest blade of grass to the creator-god—is maya. According to him such concepts as "positive" and "negative" are themselves based on maya, as are all other perceived pairs of opposites, all duality. It is because of this mysterious power of Brahman that the one appears as the many, that is, the one Self or Atman as innumerable separate living entities.

Shankara does not employ the maya concept to explain the world of phenomena and experience, but to explain it *away*. The pronouncement that the phenomenal world is maya does not explain it, after all, but simply says that it— or rather the fact that there seems to exist, in addition to the one, a multiplicity of separate entities—is not something that can be explained. Maya is the unknowable in this equation and in a sense even reflects a kind of surrender, something seemingly close to agnosticism. (Is not the central message in Shankara's voluminous work that nothing can be asserted about Nirguna Brahman and that the relative world is not something that can be determined to be either real or non-real?)

Yet this surrender differs greatly from that of the agnostic who believes the truth to be all but unattainable. Shankara, by contrast, knew himself to be in the full possession of absolute truth and loudly proclaimed it everywhere he went. One detects no hesitation in his voice; he always speaks with great authority. But although in doing so he made full use of his keen intellect, it is evident that he derived his certainty not so much from mental exertion as

from his own profound spiritual experience of what the
scriptures reveal.

The mind brightened by enlightenment serves merely as a
lamp for others on the way to liberation—it is never used as
an instrument for *explaining* the world and its phenomena.
In most of his writings Shankara avoids establishing any
connection between maya and the highest Brahman and
thus to attribute a "meaning" to Creation; he is in fact as
radically *salvation*-oriented as any Buddhist. Rather than
philosophizing about the world, he wants to help man to
free himself from delusions about it. This is particularly
true of his shorter treatises. In his commentaries on the
Brahma Sutras and the Upanishads, on the other hand, he
often goes into more detail. Here, in his attempts to prove
the correctness of orthodoxy when provoked by chal-
lengers from other philosophical schools, he grapples with
questions that are often no longer exclusively concerned
with man's salvation. He himself saw a certain danger in
this when he wrote in the Vivekacudamani (Jewel of Discrimination): "Skill in words, in expounding the scriptures,
and likewise erudition, bring satisfaction to the scholar, but
they do not bring about liberation. . . . Studying the scriptures is useless so long as the highest truth is not known,
and it is also useless when the highest truth is known. . . .
Consisting of many words, the scriptures are like a dense
forest: they cause the mind to wander aimlessly about. . . .
Thus a wise man strives to know the true nature of the
Self. . . . For one bitten by the serpent of ignorance there is
only one remedy: the knowledge of Brahman. . . . Of what
avail could be the Vedas and other scriptures, mantras,
medicines and the like to such a one?" (58–61)

If Shankara nevertheless from time to time yields to questions concerning the nature of maya, he defines it as neither existing nor non-existing. He likens it to a mirage which, although "there," is not something truly real. In a certain sense maya is nearly as mysterious as Brahman, which also defies description. Where this maya-mirage obtains—and for most people it is very much *there*—it is not only taken for real but also for the totality of reality. Yet the moment enlightenment occurs the whole mirage vanishes in a flash. The comparison with someone waking from a dream is obvious. We may laugh about it afterward. Over and over in Vedanta literature we find enlightenment and illusion compared to a rope taken for a snake in insufficient light. For the person experiencing this, the illusionary snake is very real indeed—but in bright light the imagined snake is instantly revealed to be just a rope.

Occasionally, almost as a concession, Shankara refers to Brahman as the very basis for the phenomenal world. Without this basis, without the existence of an absolute reality, one could not speak of an illusion about it. The illusion of the snake is possible only because of the real presence of a rope. It is not only because maya has made us blind that we mistake the world of common experience for all there is to reality, but also because the Brahman is indeed supporting it all.

"*Sat-chit-ananda* [Being-Consciousness-Bliss] is present in the cosmos, in air, fire, water, and earth, as much as in devas, animals and man. . . . Through *nama-rupa* [name-and-form] they are distinguished one from the other," it says in the Drg-Drsya-Viveka (often, but probably incorrectly, ascribed to Shankara). This means that insofar as the phenomenal world has the first three attributes in common with Brahman, it is grounded in reality. What distin-

guishes it from Brahman and what distinguishes one thing
from another is nama-rupa. Man's habit to see the world in
terms of the names he gives to things is what gives the world
its maya character. The Vedantic mystic aims at doing
away with this veil of names and forms which we superim-
pose on reality, hence blocking our view of the "thing-in-
itself." Nama-rupa is responsible for our viewing this
world as an independent reality, as something separate
from, or outside of, Brahman—the truly one-without-
a-second. Once enlightenment is attained this "world" disappears.

But, we may ask, does it really disappear altogether—or
does it then reveal itself in its pure Brahman state? Or are
they perhaps both the same?

THE SWORD OF DISCRIMINATING INSIGHT

For the most part Shankara does not go into the above
question. He probably wanted to keep his disciples from
conjecturing too much about the view from the summit
while they were still at the foot of the mountain. As we said
before, he taught a way of salvation, one that would free
man from the grip of maya and eventually lead him to
realization of the highest Brahman.

However, this emphasis on salvation and liberation also
caused the practicing yogi, as well as the philosopher (who
simply won't go away), to use the Sword of Discriminating
Knowledge (*viveka*) to battle his way through to final oneness. And discrimination first of all presupposes a duality.
Probably one of the greatest difficulties the reader of Advaita texts encounters is the ever-present specter of duality

conjured up in the name of ultimate oneness: clear distinctions are always made between Brahman and maya, between eternal being and temporal becoming, between Self and non-Self, between the one who does the seeing and the object seen. Anyone fleeing from the endless dualisms of the intellectual culture of the West—whether of Platonic or Cartesian imprint—who expectantly turns to the East in the hope of discovering there at last the oneness its wisdom is reputed to be centered on, is bound to be irritated in the beginning by what seems like a veritable passion for discrimination. (It is actually quite typical of Indian thinking, while China, being rather un-Platonic and down-to-earth, has by and large remained faithful to an ideal of wholeness in its thinking.) Thus, in the Vedanta of Shankara, instead of finding the long-sought-after "Jewel of Oneness," he first comes upon his *Jewel of Discrimination*. Of course, it soon dawns on him that with this weapon of duality Shankara is actually heading straight for non-duality: for however paradoxical it may sound, it is precisely duality that he is combating with the Sword of Discriminating Insight.

The price to be paid for achieving oneness, then, is that portion of reality to which the average human applies this term. This is the part that is swept off the table, is "discriminated." "Brahman alone is real," Shankara categorically declares, "all else is false." But what exactly is this "all else," here so decisively done away with, and which is not to be conceived of as existing outside of or in addition to Brahman as "a second"? Well, it is practically everything: the entire Creation along with the creator. All that remains and is tolerated is one sole reality, something so ineffable—such pure being—that one can almost refer to it as "nothing."

Presumably Shankara experienced no problems at all in

the state of *samadhi* (deepest immersion in meditation) even as a philosophical thinker. He joyfully exclaims in the Vivekacudamani, for instance: "In the ocean of Absolute Bliss, what is there to be rejected or accepted, what else is there than the Self, what distinct from It?" (484) Yet in the very next verse he says: "[In that state] I neither see nor hear nor know anything. I am the Atman, Bliss Eternal, different from everything else." (485)

In the first verse we seem to have someone enlightened before us, someone for whom nothing "else" exists, just the sea of Brahman where no distinctions obtain. In the second verse, however, this Vedantic teaching of oneness takes on marked Sankhya-yoga features: the enlightened yogi conceives of himself as the eternal subject, different from "all else," from prakriti. In the splendid isolation of one who has cut off all attachments, he is "the one."

This contradiction runs through all of Shankara's work and is particularly noticeable in his *Jewel of Discrimination*. One almost suspects Shankara of having deliberately inserted *koans* (Zen paradoxes) into the text in order to tease our overly logical mind—were it not for other passages where he very much indeed insists on logic, in fact so much so that we begin to long for the more poetical paradoxes of the Upanishads again where it is simply stated, for instance, that "[the Atman] though sitting still, It travels far; though lying down, It goes everywhere" (Katha Upanishad, I.ii.21), without explaining this paradox in terms of a two-level theory according to which the Atman has two aspects: one at rest and one in motion (the latter being ultimately illusionary for Shankara). As long as Advaita remains cheerfully sublime above human logic, there is no problem; but when, as with Shankara, it presents itself as a system in conflict with other philosophical systems, certain difficulties and weaknesses become apparent.

MAYA AND EVIL

Viewed historically, Shankara's maya-concept seems to belong to a long series of philosophical doctrines that radically separate absolute being—synonymous with truth—from the world of becoming and passing away, the latter of which was declared to be more or less unreal or untrue. In Greek philosophy this orientation was represented above all by Parmenides and the Eleatics. In the school of Plato and in neo-Platonism this tendency continued to exist in modified form, eventually leaving a decisive mark on medieval theology. As indicated earlier, metaphysical ideas and ethical values interpenetrated each other here. It is not by mere chance that in Sanskrit the words for being (*sat*) and truth (*satya*) are linguistically almost identical. For a Shankara, as for a St. Thomas Aquinas, changeless, eternal being is equivalent to the Good and the True. All else is in a sense non-being, delusion, however convincing and self-righteous it may look. Being is what is not subject to change, what is timeless and eternal; while what changes, comes and goes, is born and dies, is not only transitory and in the deepest sense unreal, but, because it is based on false perceptions, also "wrong" and therefore in need of salvation.

Although maya cannot simply be identified with evil (for it is both darkness *and* light, and thus also the twilight which characterizes our relative existence between being

and non-being), the constant battle these Vedanta philosophers, particularly Shankara, waged against this metaphysical monster nevertheless recalls in a great many ways
the wrestling of the doctors of the Christian church with
the devil. Shankara-the-philosopher even dons the armor of
a St. George when it comes to battling the gunas of prakriti
and the maya-caused sensation of separateness and inde-
pendence: egoism. "The treasure of the Bliss of Brahman is
held in the coils of the mighty and terrible serpent of egoism, with its three fierce heads, the gunas, constantly on
guard. Only the wise who sever the three heads with the
mighty Sword of Realization in accordance with the teachings of the shrutis, enjoy this treasure which confers infinite
bliss," we read in the Vivekacudamani. (302)

Neither the Vedanta philosophers nor the Fathers of the
Christian church have an easy time when it comes to finding the cause of maya or evil. St. Thomas Aquinas, for
example, begins with the bold statement that "the cause of
evil is the Good," but continues, ". . . insofar as evil can
have a cause at all. For one must know that evil cannot have
an actual cause."[12]

We are fed similar philosophical koan exercises in Vedanta. In both cases the first principle that applies is that,
ultimately, everything must have its cause in the nature of
the divine since no second source exists beside God, such
as, for instance, an independent evil principle or any independently existing original matter outside Brahman. Both
Shankara and St. Thomas are so convinced of the absolute
sovereignty of this one divine being that they would rather
blame the existence of evil—or the exceedingly various
features of maya—on this higher being, than to assume any
other source.

St. Thomas Aquinas then gets out of the problem by stating that, fundamentally, evil has no cause at all. How can this be? Something without a cause is, after all, either identical with the divine being—which is self-generated, so to speak—or else it is non-being, that is, "nothing." St. Thomas resorts to this line of reasoning when he says (clearly following St. Augustine), "Evil consists entirely in non-being."[13] Of course, one need not look for a cause for non-being. But then again he says, "No matter how much evil be multiplied, it can never destroy the good wholly."[14] While this is certainly comforting, it also seems rather odd that "non-being" has the capacity to expand and at least partially cover the good (that is, true being). A comparison with maya suggests itself here, for although maya is denied any final reality by the Vedanta philosophers, it nevertheless seems to have this capacity to conceal Brahman to the point where we are no longer able to see through it and perceive the *oneness* of reality.

How can this contradiction be resolved? Theologians and philosophers, whether in the West or in India, would scarcely have devoted so many pages to a negative power if they entirely denied its existence. Rather, it seems that they admit its *empirical* existence. Evil, or for that matter maya, is not real in the sense that absolute being is, but at the same time not totally unreal. It is there, one has to reckon and grapple with it. At every turn we are being warned of the ingenious snares of the devil or of maya. What for the religious practitioner can be quite tangible becomes for the ontologist and metaphysician an almost insurmountable problem. One can categorically proclaim that Brahman alone is "true" and all else is "false," yet one seems thereby also to be indirectly conceding again that there indeed *is* this "all else," this "shadow" of Brahman that is said to be "false" or "unreal." What causes this mysterious "all else," this additional something that is not supposed to be there and is clouding our perception of the one reality? Where does this enigmatic maya, this shimmering display between being and nothing, come from? Since Brahman is the sole reality, it can really only have its origin in Brahman itself—insofar as it has any cause at all. For it is important to know that in truth—And here the mind begins to overheat.

It is no accident that the discursive intellect always runs into a brick wall at this point—it itself belongs, after all, to the realm of maya. For this reason, too, the mind can never free itself from maya. All explanations regarding its nature are necessarily part and parcel of it. Maya is time, space, and causality, and is why we ask questions in the first place. Thus the question as to where maya "comes from" is unanswerable. And fortunately—or unfortunately—there is no other maya outside maya.

We can see that the question concerning the nature of maya leads us to broader and deeper regions than the question about the existence of evil does—which in a way deals only with the *ethical* aspect of the problem with a metaphysical touch. Vedanta is more concerned with the *metaphysical* aspect—with here and there a touch of ethics. Shankara does not exercise his mind over why someone commits adultery or breaks someone's neck in a world created by God as "good." Instead, he is puzzling out how it comes about that man perceives only a multiplicity of transient phenomena, where really only the *one* exists. He probably regrets as much as anyone else the horrible and hair-raising things that happen in this maya-world, but it is not his mission to rid the world of any particular evil. For the Vedantin, good and evil are part of the very structure of this maya-world, consisting as it does of all kinds of dualisms, of so many pairs of opposites. It is precisely duality and multiplicity—sources of eternal "duel-ling" and discord—he wants to eliminate. He wants the entire universe as we see it to disappear—to make room for the *one*, which until then is concealed by the *many*.

The sage, dwelling fully in the *one*, scarcely ever permits himself to be drawn into philosophical debate, for he would thus get involved in the realm of maya again and therefore be subject to its laws. So why, then, did Shankara still philosophize; why did he continually battle real or even imaginary opponents?

Someone as enlightened as Shankara has really only two choices: either he remains completely silent or he fights maya, in the realm of maya, and with the weapons of maya. Our thinking is so dependent on opposites that even the idea of oneness needs the contrasting image of two-ness, or duality, in order to come into clear focus. Thus something which can really never be the subject of knowledge is made an object one can think *about*. The smiling sage firmly established in oneness becomes on a somewhat lower plane, we might say, a sort of missionary for oneness, a knight fighting the dragon of maya. As soon as this many-headed monster raises one of its heads, he is there to cut it off. He cuts off everything: sensation and volition, emotion and the flickerings of the mind—in short, all stirrings of prakriti (Nature), even eventually ideas of heavenly regions and the creator-god himself (since even they are only a maya-picture of the absolute). There is only one thing this high-minded knight occasionally forgets in the course of his battles: that, ultimately, his efforts are also maya—because *any* differentiation is maya. In the course of all this, however, we learn to recognize some of our grossest errors; we

learn that our idea of a separate "I" is wrong, that there are
not innumerable separate selves, but in truth only one Self.
But because this *one* is still differentiated from multiplicity
in order to be an object of thought, we, along with Shankara, still have at least one foot in maya, in dualistic con-
ceptualization. Even the absolute is maya when it is thought
of in terms of the opposite of what is relative. So long as we
feel the need to "protect" Brahman from maya it is not total
reality.

In the Upanishads, Brahman was not yet separate from
his Shakti, his creative omnipotence. There it was enough
to say, "Brahman projects the universe through the power
of Its maya. In that universe Brahman is entangled through
maya." (Svetasvatara Upanishad, IV.9) We might say that
man was in those times still living in the paradise of an
undivided mind, and that at least in the older Upanishads
he had not yet taken such a big bite from the fruit of
knowledge based on discrimination. Shankara, on the
other hand, lived in a "fallen" world still bearing the imprint of Jainism, Buddhism, and Sankhya-yoga. He needed
first of all to reestablish oneness philosophically. Furthermore, to preclude the risk of a naive pantheism eventually
growing out of this process of differentiation, he elevated
Brahman to such heights that it no longer really had much
to do with the phenomenal world of Creation. Only when
Vedanta's prestige was on the line (in the course of the
debates between the various philosophical schools) did he
reject the dualism of the Sankhya system and return to
Upanishadic formulations, that is, that the whole universe
is a manifestation of the highest Self. In his role as defender
of the one divine Nature he does not even hesitate to act like
a monotheist. But we already know that he is playing this
role only on the relative plane. He immediately rein-

troduces the maya concept, thereby taking back the idea of a direct manifestation. Still, in order not to fall back into the trap of dualism, he also invests maya with what he calls "the Power of the Lord"—thereby surely intending to make it clear that maya is no evil power in opposition to God—or for that matter any neutral, independently existing reality. However, he also declares war on maya with the zeal of one fighting the devil himself.

THE MAYA CONCEPT

The contradictions mentioned in the previous chapter should, however, not be blamed on Shankara alone; they are inherent in the very structure of our twilight existence which is at once divine and non-divine. The maya concept may in the case of the Shankara school have led to a one-sidedly negative worldview, but when we look at it more closely the maya teaching turns out to be quite useful.

According to the Vedanta teaching, maya can obscure and conceal as well as project. Its concealing aspect is associated primarily with the guna of tamas (ignorance, darkness, inertia), its projecting aspect with rajas (activity). Yet it is not that maya at one time only conceals, at another only projects. Rather, it is precisely the paradoxical nature of maya that through its very revealing it conceals and through its many masks it reveals. Without concealment there is, after all, no revelation. The "golden disk" in the Isha Upanishad reveals the beauty of the divine, yet at the same time hides the truth. The mask expresses what is behind it—yet at the same time thereby conceals the "true face." (15, 16)

For a better understanding of the maya-concept, let us

also consider similarities it has with certain Western ideas, for instance the famous words of St. Paul: "For now we see through a glass, darkly, but then face to face. Now I only know in part, but then shall I know, even as also I am known." (I.Cor.13:12) Just as the small smoky glass or mirror of ancient times could not give a true image, so the veil of maya obscures the truth.

Or we could think of maya as a hall of many mirrors where, to our amusement as well as bewilderment, we lose track of ourselves as we really are. It is not as though reality had suddenly vanished then, but that we catch only reflections, bits and pieces of it. Like the image of an object under water, the truth is often curiously distorted. (The world of maya is both a vale of tears and a hall-of-many-mirrors-and-laughter.)

Although there are also more positive revelations of God in the relative domain, such as certain symbols, images, or miracles, they too are still maya, even if divine: we are still seeing divine reality "through a glass darkly." Even the purest image—God's Word become flesh, or OM mani-fest—becomes an obstacle on the way if we let outer appearances prevent us from pressing on to what underlies them, on to where we are "face to face with God." Only when the thinnest veil of maya has vanished "shall I know, even as also I am known then." Eventually the beholder becomes one with what he beholds, the knowing subject and the object of his understanding become one. To quote the radical "Advaitin," Meister Eckhart, again: "The eye in which I behold God is the same eye in which God sees me. My eye and God's eye they are one eye and one seeing and one knowing and one loving." While St. Paul may not have envisioned this oneness quite so radically as Shankara, but may have equated the above "then" with a future state after death and not with enlightenment in this life, the principle is very similar: the way leads from the relative to the absolute.

While such pioneers of modern physics as Einstein with his Theory of Relativity, and Heisenberg with his Probability Principle, can give us some insight into Eastern thinking, Western man tends on the whole more toward sharply defined either/or positions. Either something is true or it is false. When one first comes across Shankara's Advaita Vedanta one may think that this same mentality existed there, too—even quite strongly—since a sharp distinction is made repeatedly and often with great zeal between a "true" Brahman and a "false" maya-world—but there it pertains only to *appearances*. We are not dealing with total falsity or complete ignorance, but with a lower or relative level of knowledge. Psychologically, it is perhaps understandable that someone who has at last managed the plunge into the absolute, later refers to all previously held half-truths as "lies" and to twilight as "darkness," or that a spiritual guide finds it expedient to paint things black and white; but we generally find a marked feel for the relative in the East, expressed there mainly in terms of different levels or stages of understanding the truth. A Vedantin can, for example, almost fanatically defend the teaching of reincarnation vis-à-vis a Western Christian—then declare calmly a minute later that, ultimately, this teaching also is only maya. In so doing, however, he does not declare it to be false, but only says something like: this teaching has only relative validity; it is valid only in the realm of space, time, and causality— that is to say, in maya—but in truth there is no such thing as reincarnation since in the timeless ground of the divine where we are eternally "suspended" there is no individual soul wandering about in search of perfection.

The relative nature of maya becomes nevertheless the undoing of anyone too eagerly battling maya and trying to play off the absolute against it. It is precisely here where maya can still make even the absolute seem like something relative—insofar as we see the latter only as the opposite of the former. But even the idea of such a contrast as absolute/ relative is maya. Similarly, anyone referring to maya as "lower" will eventually have to accept that such concepts as "high" and "low" are maya to begin with—as are indeed all concepts. There is nothing "she" has not caused. To be sure, she is not the cause of the attributeless Nirguna Brahman. But then again, separating the two—however brilliantly argued, as in the case of Shankara—can also only be her doing. It is, therefore, not really surprising when Shankara pays due respect to maya when he says: "She is neither existent, nor non-existent, nor both; neither same, nor different, nor both; neither composed of parts, nor an indivisible whole, nor both. . . ." (Vivekacudamani, 109) This description is almost identical with descriptions of Nirguna Brahman or Nagarjuna's "emptiness." Anyone who has taken the last dialectical leap to realization no longer separates *nirvana* and *samsara:* he sees the "great inexplicable" (maya) and the "great inexpressible" (Nirguna Brahman) as *not-two.*

Nevertheless, as far as the disciple still treading along the path is concerned, there is no harm in his taking the warnings about maya seriously. Mere intellectual cleverness will not advance his cause. The "strands" which bind us *are* very strong, the human mind *is* very unsteady (as Arjuna, for instance, exclaims in the Gita), and the web of names and forms (nama-rupa) which we spin over reality—over things as they are in and of themselves—is very real indeed. Each one of us, in a way, is spinning his own maya-cocoon, each one has his or her own view of reality. We might say that the great cosmic maya-game consists in innumerable subjective daydreams. It is no mere coincidence that all great religious teachers call on us to *awaken*.

ADVAITA AND YOGA

It is because of human instability that Vedanta, in practice, became bound up with the yoga system—more specifically with the classical raja-yoga of Patanjali—which teaches a gradual release from the fetters, or strands, of prakriti through increasing degrees of detachment. Mental exercises, such as the withdrawal of the senses (pratyahara), concentration (dharana), meditation (dyana), and their culmination in the final state of absorption (samadhi) are already mentioned in many of the Upanishads, in the Gita, and, of course, in the later Advaita Vedanta texts.

However, a frequent subject of polemical elaborations in Advaita literature, such as the rather radical Ashtavakra Samhita, is the subtle difference that exists between yoga and Vedanta. A typical raja-yogi, for instance, relies primarily on systematic *exercises*—he literally "works" for his own benefit—for him everything is an experiment the final "result" of which is samadhi. The Vedantic jnani, on the other hand—no matter how many yoga exercises he may adopt—never loses sight of the truth that the real heart of liberation consists in the knowledge that he already *is*, and has always been, Brahman, that is, that there is in effect nothing really to *do*. Vedantic "exercise" centers on remembering our everlasting Atman nature. The Vedanta teacher merely whispers the truth into the disciple's ear: "Tat tvam asi" (That thou art). Looked at from this perspective, Vedanta has actually more in common with Zen than with classical yoga, where the emphasis is on step-by-step advancement.

It is therefore not surprising that many Advaita texts read very much like irreverent Zen texts. "Meditation and control of the mental functions, all these things only cause confusion. In knowledge I rest firmly within the Self," we read in the Ashtavakra Samhita. The point of this book seems to be that we should not become attached to anything—and certainly not to meditation and enlightenment—but just be content. Of course, at the outset, classical yoga as well as Vedanta insists on the gradual detachment from the senses, from mental activity, and from the phenomena of the "world." Along with such detachment eventually comes freedom from anxious clinging to this or that particular dogma or school.

In the end the systematic yoga path is transcended—the very effort to achieve enlightenment is ridiculed—and even the highest "truths" of Vedanta, to the extent to which they remain stuck at the conceptual level, are called into question. Someone who still has to keep hammering it into his head that he is the Brahman and quite different from the "world" may be on the way, but has surely not yet reached the goal. "For the Self dwelling beyond the world of desire, where is delusion, where the universe, where renunciation, where liberation?" (XVIII. 14)

With these and similar rhetorical questions the Ashtavakra Samhita tries again and again to force the reader to abandon accustomed categories of thought. But is liberation not the final goal one should strive for? Certainly. Only, in the final analysis, *it* also is still something relative, that is to say dependent on the opposite idea of a bound and ignorant self. For someone truly liberated such contrasting opposites no longer obtain. He is neither attached to action nor to inaction; he neither lusts for life nor despises it. He has gone beyond such concepts as knowledge and ignorance. "Fools desire peace of mind through control of the mind and thus never achieve it. The sage knows the Truth and thus has peace of mind." (XVIII. 39) To the yogi, desperately trying to escape the round of birth-and-death, the following deliberately provocative statement is addressed: "The sage neither despises death nor does he strive to realize the Self. Free from joy and sorrow, he is neither dead nor alive." (XIII. 83) In other words, the relative states of dream, dreamless sleep, and waking have vanished—along with the "fourth" state (turiya)—no relative: therefore no absolute. Transcendence is at last transcended. "Where is awakening to transcendent reality or where the state of being an unenlightened fool . . . where is the Self, and where the non-Self . . . where is the pupil, where the teacher . . . where the many, where the one. . . ." (XIX.9, 4, 13)

This is true a-dvaita, which is by no means confined to Vedanta. We find this peculiar and unmistakable logic in the literature of Indian Mahayana Buddhism, in Tibetan texts such as *Saraha's Treasure of Songs*, in the *Zen Teachings of Huang-Po*, and in the many sayings of our own Meister Eckhart. These are lofty heights and the mystics who find themselves there all seem to be a little mad. It might be that these heights represent the utmost in human spiritual emancipation—yet the "emancipated" mystic himself seems unaware of anything he is emancipated *from*. He is not part of some elite, either. He has long left behind such notions as "high" and "low." Who is enlightened, who is unenlightened! He dwells beyond knowledge and ignorance; and even if one of them occasionally slips into the role of philosopher, it should be equally possible to spot another one, broom in hand, vigorously cleaning a downtown street.

Still, we ought not forget that these sages began by taking for granted what they eventually came to laugh at. They seem to have ended up in a no-man's-land, a grand, joy-filled "emptiness"—but they did not set out from there. They seem to have little use for philosophy and religion, yet they represent the pinnacle of both for having transcended them. They are not voices of dissent, but, having pushed beyond conceptual limits and at last come down from their fancy flights of mind and spirit, they are "the naked," "the poor of the spirit." In the end they found what they had never lost, what they had always been. They did not "get" anything. Yet this seems precisely what makes them so happy and cheerful.

SUMMARY OF THE MAYA-TEACHING

Let us in conclusion look once more at the Advaita philosophical system, this many-storied edifice on the roof of which the enlightened mystics frolic in total freedom, even shaking its foundations a little. As we said, the architect of this Vedantic construction was primarily Shankara Acharya (Shankara the Teacher). He actually, however, only rearranged various already existing elements and in the course of this gave the resulting structure his own special imprint, henceforth known as the Mayavada. Notwithstanding a great many decidedly bold formulations in Shankara's writings, however, and although he celebrated, in words that have since become "traditional," the *jivanmukta* (the one enlightened-while-yet-alive) as a "holy madman, with no thought of the morrow and looking with indifference upon the present . . ." (Vivekacudamani, 432), he himself was too much the scholar and "theologian" to join in the more freewheeling ways of these ultimate sages. Perhaps it was his role as founder and abbot of several orders and monasteries that kept this "wild" aspect within bounds.

But then again, Shankara was not at all just the dry schoolmaster many would make of him. He can be likened to St. Thomas Aquinas (who was also far more than just a scholastic and who should not be confused with the later Thomists who forged his insights into a school of thought), and to Meister Eckhart. For despite much that is dry in Shankara's writings, they also reflect his genius, his all-encompassing vision and active commitment. One can also not help but admire his gift for language, the clarity and poetic power acknowledged even by those in India who do not share his philosophical views. Since these views constitute for many people inside and outside India the very heart of Vedanta, we shall summarize them here once more.

For Shankara only *one* reality ultimately exists: the impersonal and attributeless Nirguna Brahman. For some reason, however, this one reality does not have the *appearance* of a seamless whole but of a plurality of separate entities: a personal god (Ishvara), a world (*jagat*) and countless individual embodied souls (*jivas*). Shankara calls this phenomenon and its potential power *maya*. Like a mirage, maya cannot be said to exist or not to exist, to be light or darkness, to be good or evil. As prakriti, maya is the womb of Nature, the origin of all form (including divine ones) and also what makes the visible universe seem object-like and something we can divide into constituent parts and analyze. As Shakti, maya has a more positive connotation as the creative (female) energy and omnipotence of the Lord of the Universe (Ishvara), who with her help projects the universe out of himself. In a more philosophical sense, however, maya is in Shankara's system only a temporary aid, not unlike the unknown X in an equation which, while contributing to its solution, has no intrinsic reality of its own. To the extent that Shankara, as heir to the Upanishads, bases his system on the Brahman, it is quite clear, but to the extent it depends on the aid of this complex maya-construct, it is as full of contradictions as the concept itself. Perhaps it is better to humbly address maya as the Divine Mother, as Ramakrishna did, than to wrestle with the concept philosophically, for it is bound to be a losing battle: maya has never been vanquished by the human intellect, not even with the Sword of Discrimination, for it is itself the cause of intellection and differentiation.

At the lower level, Shankara had a place for devotion to Saguna Brahman (Ishvara), the personal god with attributes, and is even said to have encouraged the performance of Hindu ritual, while, however, having rejected its more extreme sectarian trends. Vishnu, Krishna, Shiva, or Durga are only maya-aspects of the one god. In his monastic communities he is said to have introduced the worship of Durga, the mother goddess.

On this relative plane Shankara also allowed a distinc-

tion between God and the individual soul; for while the
Lord Ishvara is master over maya, the individual soul is at
this stage still a captive of maya and must strive from birth
to free itself from this imprisonment in time, space, and
causality. For purposes of purifying the spirit, Shankara
attributed a certain importance to karma-yoga (the Path of
Action) and bhakti-yoga (the Path of Loving Devotion to
God), although characteristically, he defined bhakti as
"man's search for his true nature." (Vivekacudamani, 31)
Yet, however many beautiful hymns to the various Hindu
deities Shankara composed during his short life, the path of
all paths for him remained the path of jnana, of absolute
knowledge. Even when he presented himself as a bhakta,
his love for a divine "Thou" never quite reached the fervor
of a St. Francis, a Chaitanya, or a Ramakrishna.

Although Shankara's works are laced with the usual ascetic advice and psychological suggestions, his ultimate
statement is to the effect that the highest knowledge can
be attained only through realization in enlightenment. For
Shankara, there are no *means* by which one can achieve this
knowledge, there is no *path* to this realization—only the
sudden onset of the experience of reality in its unadulte-
rated form.

But Shankara also knew that this realization, which enables man to be one with his Brahman nature in the ever-
present *now,* requires a certain amount of preparation.
At the relative level he therefore affirmed the Hindu belief
in reincarnation: the wandering of the individual soul
through many forms of existence until it rids itself of all
erroneous identifications with its sheaths, its bodily "enve-
lope," and realizes its original boundlessness again. Because it is only in its human embodiment that the soul can
seek and realize the Self (Atman), Shankara calls one who

does not use this condition as a springboard to realization of the Atman, but instead continues to cling to a false reality, a fool.

Among the qualifications a candidate must possess, according to Shankara, are: the ability to distinguish between things permanent and transient; renunciation of any reward in the here or the hereafter; and the fervent desire to be liberated. He must further cultivate inner calmness, control of the senses, mental stability, forbearance and concentration, loving surrender and confidence. Although, at the moment of enlightenment, ideas like "bondage" and "liberation" prove to be illusory, the desire for release remains the motivating force along the way to attaining the state of illusionlessness.

Shankara named Vedic revelation, reason, and direct experience as the three pillars supporting the spiritual truth of Vedanta and said this truth is guaranteed by the harmony of all three. Since Shankara saw all of reality as one, this harmony was a foregone conclusion for him. (Whenever there were loose ends in his logic, Shankara just cut them off—all for the sake of this harmonious *one*.)

Concerning the phenomenal world as it relates to Brahman, Shankara was basically in tune with the radical teaching of "non-arising" of his teacher Gaudapada, which in turn has much in common with the Doctrine of the Void (shunyata) of Nagarjuna, founder of the Madhyamika school of Mahayana Buddhism. According to this philosophy, one cannot really speak of the existence or non-existence of the phenomenal world, nor that it is subject to origination and cessation. In Nagarjuna's words: "nothing coming in, nothing going out." (Astasa-hsrika Prajnaparamita, 18) By denying *all* antithetical assertions, all cause-and-effect arguments are reduced to absurdity and made to look ludicrous.

As creator of a philosophical work of great complexity, which also compelled him to devote much of his attention to the refutation of many other philosophical doctrines of his time, however, Shankara was rarely this radical and unambiguous. He cites three main causes for anything being "there" at all: Brahman, illusion (maya), and lacking knowledge (*ajnana*) or personal ignorance (*avidya*). With regard to the first, Shankara follows the older Upanishads by explaining the world as the outflowing and superabundance of Brahman, as universal being, beyond all mere *being there*. This is the explanation of the origination of the world "from on high," so to speak. Shankara could not have called himself spiritual heir to the Upanishads if he had not suggested this view, allowing for the world's origin in the divine.

But similar to the Buddhists, he also explained the phenomenal world "from below," so to speak, as the result of human ignorance and attachment which, since time immemorial, have kept the cycle of birth-and-death going by super-imposition; that is, by "the seeing of a thing in something which is not that." (Shankara's commentary on the Brahma Sutras, I.i.1–4) Thus, where there is no ignorance and no attachment, there is also no such world, and no ripple on the calm sea of Brahman; there simply would be no fuel to maintain such an illusory world. While the Tree of the Universe (symbolized by an Indian fig tree with air roots) has its roots in the Upanishads and the Gita—that is "up high"—Shankara calls ignorance the very seed of this tree. (Vivekacudamani, 145) Many of his pronouncements in this connection relate to this subjectivity, as when he writes: "Outside the mind, not-knowing and ignorance do not exist. The mind alone does not know, and causes the bondage of transmigration. When it disappears, all else disappears; when it arises, all else arises." (Vivekacudamani, 196) In the next verse Shankara describes the entire phenomenal world as a "projection of the human mind." While this is only *one* strand in Shankara's argumentation—and many other passages could be quoted where he attacks just this kind of argument and allows a certain objective reality, independent of the human mind—it is also true that it is an integral component of Shankara's view of the relative world. It has received even greater stress by later adherents of Advaita Vedanta, so much so, in fact, that it is generally regarded as characteristic of this school.

As for the explanation which focuses on maya as the origin of the world, we could think of it as linking these two extremes. For while expressly calling maya the "creative power of the Lord"—which may seem like explaining origination "from on high"—the very notion of any creative activity was for Shankara illusory and therefore a fall from true being, from Nirguna Brahman, which is "forever tranquil and without actions." Thus we are back in the questionable realm of maya, "down there" with human ignorance and craving—however magnificent and impressive the "achievements" of this creative power of the Lord often may appear to be. But since ignorance is itself an aspect of maya, its subjective factor so to speak, it may be said to be driving the world of phenomena "from below."

Shankara stressed, above all, the negative aspects of maya. For him, only the one immutable Brahman reality existed, the oneness of all being, not innumerable forms which he brushed aside as nama-rupa. He was not interested in the great variety of shapes and forms pottery comes in, but their common property: clayness. This often-quoted comparison suggests a monism which sees Brahman as the immaterial substratum of the world. For Shankara, the true reality of every specific form resides in its intrinsic Brahman nature (Atman), not in its special characteristics which are subject to change and dissolution and therefore as unreal as images in a dream. The strange paradox running through Shankara's entire system is that, while Brahman alone constitutes the reality and meaning of every individual form, it is at the same time what deprives it of independent reality and meaning. *Meaning and meaninglessness converge.* On the one hand Brahman is what "supports" the manifold universe in that it permeates all things with its being, its consciousness and its bliss, and on the other it so completely permeates it that it reduces the relative world to nought.

To someone creative who views form and giving a particular shape to things as something decidedly positive, all this does not have a very encouraging ring. Shankara's absolute does not seem to include any creative impulse, but rather to absorb any and all creative initiative. Although Shankara-the-philosopher presents his teaching with a certain poetic verve, particularly in his smaller works, the sole purpose of all this is, after all, to free us from the grip of maya, this fashioner of illusion, this artist par excellence. In the end we are left with a certain grandiose monotony. Clear and well reasoned—and not even altogether joyless—as these texts are, one may question whether this Advaita (which revels in blissful release, but squarely rejects as maya the realm of Shakti, the creative power of Brahman) really qualifies as non-duality. One senses the danger of an intellectual rigidity, sterility and one-sidedness. With Shankara, this one-sidedness still had the touch of genius about it, but under the systematizers who followed him it became ever more problematic.

Defending the Citadel of God: Love of the Personal God

IN THE FOREGOING CHAPTER we said that at the lower level of his philosophical system Shankara "tolerated" the worship of a personal god. This is, however, not to say that the great jnani looked on the personal god Ishvara only as a concession to the faith of simple folk, as mere superstition, something he would laugh at in private. With all his crypto-Buddhist tendencies Shankara was indeed a theist: he acknowledged a supreme being not subject to the Law of Karma and the bonds of ignorance and which governed Creation by virtue of its maya. If, like our own Meister Eckhart, he thought of this god as to "appear and disappear" (lit., become and un-become), it was not in the sense that he, like the Vedic gods—from minor deities all the way up to Brahmā—took on a role for a time in the celestial hierarchy, eventually to disappear from the scene, but that in the deepest state of absorption (nirvikalpa samadhi) where no "I" and "Thou" obtain, God disappears along with the individual "I." For Shankara, as for most Hindus, there was indeed an eternally immutable Lord of the Uni-

151

verse, representing, as it were, the absolute in the realm of maya.

Shankara's impersonal Nirguna Brahman is thus not the last link in a chain of logical reasoning—the mental abstraction left after the personal god has been stripped of all attributes—but precisely the reality experienced in the state of deepest absorption. In this state, according to Shankara, there is no longer any god, just as there is no longer a world—celestial or earthly—and just as there is in that state no individual soul "beholding God." In order to make this supreme experience the cornerstone of his theological system, Shankara brought much reasoning to bear on the matter. But Shankara-the-enlightened-mystic is also often in evidence in this otherwise rather dry system—as when he proclaims that there is a plane where everything is entirely "different"; where the laws of maya no longer apply; where distinctions like subject and object fall away; where "Tat tvam asi" and "Aham brahma asmi" ("That thou art" and "I am Brahman") are actually experienced. However great Ishvara may be, he bore for Shankara only limited resemblance to that reality. Ishvara is the absolute—but seen through the veil of maya.

To be sure, only the narrow and difficult path of jnana leads to this stark and naked *one,* and not many can hold out for long in this rarified atmosphere; after all, where there is nothing but the one, no "relationship" can really be said to exist. We may ask how even religious love can exist without an "I" and "Thou"? But is love not also absolute? And if so, does it really make sense to brush aside the I/Thou relationship as merely "relative" and "provisional"? The Vedanta texts deal almost exclusively with Self and non-Self, with subject and object, and with the disappearance of these opposites in deepest absorption (samadhi). Almost never is there any mention of a personal relationship between the two, and when there is, "I" and "Thou" are made part of these pairs of opposites which vanish in samadhi. Thus something very important seems to be missing in Shankara's seemingly all-encompassing system, something which is really part of *absolute* divine nature. Shankara's Nirguna Brahman is in fact only *half* of the truth, only one side of reality. Does the other side, the personal, creative, dynamic, and above all *loving* side of God not also have a claim to absolute reality?

THE PENDULUM SWINGS BACK: RAMANUJA

When, in the centuries that followed, the representatives of a theistic Vedanta turned against Shankara's Advaita system, they did not simply ask tentative questions and meekly plead for their personal god to be taken into consideration and granted a modicum of reality. They instead went straight on the counterattack, declaring not only the personal god to *be* the absolute but also Nirguna Brahman to be a windy "nothingness," the illusion of a philosopher caught up in abstractions, and who, they said, would have done better to have gone over to the Buddhists in the first place instead of cleverly introducing their ideas into Hinduism. It made no difference to them that Shankara "tolerated" the personal god at a "lower" level; this kind of tolerance often irks a full-blooded bhakta more than any straightforward denial of God.

Through Ramakrishna, Vivekananda, and other representatives of the new Hinduism we have become accustomed to seeing Vedanta as a wide-open system with plenty of room for everything, where static and dynamic, impersonal and personal forms are merely considered different aspects of one and the same divinity. But in the Middle Ages such a synthesis was not yet in sight. At that time we only find Shankara's static absolute on the one side of the divide (with a certain tolerance of Ishvara for those who are not yet fully enlightened), and a series of theistic systems on the other, all of whom, despite many differences, shared the fundamental conviction that the personal god *is* the complete and highest absolute and in no need of being transcended for an impersonal Nirguna Brahman.

The leaders of these large-scale offensives were Ramanuja and Madhva. Like Shankara they came from the south of India, indeed exclusively from circles who worshiped the god Vishnu. From the beginning, this link with the mythology of Vaishnavism gave theistic Vedanta a somewhat one-sided character. Shaivism—the school of Shiva worshipers—went its own way and produced an important system known as Shaiva-Siddhanta. Within the larger framework of Vedanta, it was mainly elements of this Shiva-worship which combined with Advaita and the jnana-path. It is probably no coincidence that Shankara, at the "lower" level, worshiped primarily Shiva and was even considered his embodiment. Expressed in somewhat oversimplified form, we could say that if a jnani—with his strong leanings toward non-duality and an impersonal absolute—ever felt an inner need for the devotional love of a bhakta, it is above all Shiva who reflects his ideal: not the dancing Shiva, to be sure, but the god-as-ascetic, sitting in the snows of the Himalayas, meditating on his true nature.

While Shankara based his philosophy almost exclusively on the authority of the Upanishads, the Brahma Sutra, and at most the Bhagavad Gita, the theology of *theistic* Vedanta had also been influenced and to some degree formed by other textual traditions, among them the religious hymns of the Alvars—south Indian saints who expressed their bhakti feelings in fervent devotional songs; the Agamas—the sacred texts of south Indian Vaishnavism and Shaivism; the Puranas—popular tales in which philosophical problems (cosmography, for example) are dressed up in myth and where either Vishnu or Shiva is sovereign over the other deities; and the theology of the Bhagavata school— worshipers of Krishna and Vishnu—which made its presence felt in very early times in India and in a major way helped shape the worldview of the Svetasvatara Upanishad, the Bhagavad Gita, and especially the Bhagavata Purana.

Philosophical and theological debate was, however, sparked mainly by what must be the least-read and least-popular work of world religious literature: the Brahma Sutras. Also sometimes referred to as the Vedanta Sutras, they are considered by some to be *the* Vedanta texts. Many who are interested in Vedanta today feel an obligation to study them, however bothersome the task. While working one's way through these Sutras and their voluminous commentaries, it is easy to despair, and one now and then finds oneself looking out the window at the green trees outside—if only to stay in touch with the *living* Brahman.

The Brahma Sutras are usually attributed to a certain Badarayana (who in turn is identified by some Hindu traditions with the legendary Vyasa whose output must truly have been prodigious since there is little in Indian literature that he is not alleged to be responsible for). While Indian scholars date the work to before Christ (about 500 to 200 B.C.), Western scholars are inclined to put it at about

A.D. 200. However, this lack of agreement has no bearing on the nature of Brahman, the actual subject of these Sutras.

The work, which is divided into four chapters, represents the first attempt to harmonize the different ideas from the Upanishads and to bring systematic order to the perplexing variety of inspirational truths found there. This could, of course, only be brought about by a high degree of simplification; an effort at brevity which, however, left later generations with nothing but these simplified and shortened versions which eventually became inaccessible without extensive commentaries. The brief aphoristic form had become empty of recognizable content, thereby allowing every succeeding philosopher to fill this void as best he knew. It is therefore not surprising that interpretations differ greatly, that Shankara could find support for his Advaita in these Sutras while others found indications throughout to support their more theistic views.

Most agree today that the Brahma Sutras, while indeed representing a kind of "monistic" worldview (much of the polemic is directed against the dualistic Sankhya system, for example), tend generally to take the more moderate middle-path, which is actually closer to Ramanuja's philosophy than to Shankara's system.

Ramanuja (1017–1137) called his system Vishisht-Advaita. We are dealing here with a system of limited or modified non-dualism which does not sweep aside plurality as radically as Shankara's Advaita did. One could call it a "pan-en-theism," a view of God and the world which attempts to balance an extreme pantheism with a no less extreme monotheism (where the stress is on separating creator from creature). In Ramanuja's view the universe and individual souls together constitute the "body" of God, which is, however, far surpassed by God's *true* nature. But with Ramanuja this transcendent nature never turns into sheer emptiness, but retains personal features to the end. For him the personal god, Ishvara or Bhagavata, *is* the absolute—not just its shadow or maya-image. Ramanuja reproached Shankara with having unnecessarily sundered the oneness of God by having spoken of two Brahmans, one "higher" and one "lower"; he insisted that there was no mention of this in the sacred texts; that instead of two gods—one for the enlightened jnani and another for the humble bhakta—they were one and the same, and only different aspects of the same God. He maintained that when there was talk of Nirguna in these texts and Brahman was sometimes declared to be devoid of attributes, this referred only to negative attributes since God possessed only positive attributes, such as omniscience, wisdom, beauty, compassion, and so forth.

One immediately notices that these are the words of a philosopher with the heart of a bhakta. As a jnani and thinker Ramanuja felt himself quite capable of meeting the great Shankara on equal terms—he did not merely demonstrate simple purity of heart. Yet instead of thinking of jnana as the Sword of Differentiation with which to cut off everything—ultimately even the creator-god—he dedicated realization entirely to devotional love: and religious devotion is inconceivable without the personal "Thou." For this reason a trace of duality always remained: Advaita is modified to leave room for worship. As Ramakrishna was to say later: "The bhakta wants to savor sugar, not to *become* sugar." The Vedantic "Tat tvam asi" is here not taken literally as in Shankara's philosophy. The individual soul is not altogether identical with Brahman. Rather, Ramanuja's conception was that of an organic whole where the individual soul is part of Brahman. This is an intermediate position between a pure monism and a pure dualism. God is the vine and the souls are the grapes, to put it in the language of the Christian Gospel.

This idea of an organic whole in which all parts are oriented toward the one, toward God, in whose being they "partake," is not only more accessible to the human heart than Shankara's position was, but also one that makes more sense to the mind. For the mind can think only in relative terms, it sees things in relation to each other, it sees the whole and its parts. Shankara, on the other hand, expects the mind to transcend all such relative notions, including plurality, until it would reach a realm where no multitude of souls is gathered around a divine center— where the notion no longer holds that God, the world, and individual souls together "add up to the whole" of Brahman. In Shankara's Nirguna realm there is only the one, and this one is *equally* present in everything. The one *is* the many, the smallest grain of sand *is* Brahman; nothing needs to be added.

While Shankara's reasoning reached great heights and depths—and in so doing left much by the wayside— Ramanuja's was more characterized by breadth. In the colorful language of Vaishnavism, he never tired of celebrating the omniscience of his personal god. We need not go into details here concerning the mythological features of Vaishnavism. They had increased considerably since the Gita, itself rich in imagery when compared with the Upanishads. But whether one welcomes this or not, it was doubtless due to these colorful mythological features that much which would otherwise have remained hidden as the esoteric wisdom of a few rishis entered popular conscious-

ness, became incarnate there, so to speak. But as is always
the case, revelation and incarnation quickly become obscured again. God's accoutrements and the splendor of his
court soon attracted more attention than God Himself—
although this was still less true with Ramanuja. (One notes
with dismay how the ancient wisdom of the Upanishads
sometimes degenerated into this colorful religious picture-
postcard world.)

Since Ramanuja saw the sentient and non-sentient universe together as the body of God, he naturally also rebelled
against Shankara's rigorous maya-teaching. According to
him, Creation is *real* precisely because it is in a certain sense
God himself. It is not some magic trick, not merely a mirage, but part of the totality of the divine. Maya exists as
the creative power of God and impedes enlightenment only
in the lower regions: as avidya or ignorance. Typically,
Ramanuja also acknowledged this divine maya as being
manifest in the Shakti of the highest deity—in the figure of
Lakshmi, or Shri, Vishnu's devoted female consort.

One can see why Ramanuja's system did not lend itself to
being exported from India, in contrast to Shankara's much
more radical system which, eschewing imagery, made him a
celebrated philosopher in the West as well, despite his
Hindu roots. While we can relate to certain features in
Ramanuja's system—the emphasis on the individual, the
feel for an organic whole, the value placed on emotion,
especially love—these features are often encrusted with
lengthy elaborations on mythological realms, elaborations
which because of their strong Vaishnava coloring often
seem cultlike to us. The imagery is very conventional and
disappointing, especially when it comes to eschatological
ideas. No matter how much fault one may find with Shan-

kara's radical system, here one wishes for Shankara's famous sharp sword to cut off all those *vaikuntas,* those
ornate celestial regions of Vaishnavism.

Because it does not have the extra force of the maya-
doctrine, Ramanuja's system is more closed, more well-
rounded and coherent than Shankara's. While Shankara
arrives at the ultimate *one,* beyond maya, only after much
wrestling with the maya-monster, Ramanuja simply fits
everything together—the world, the individual souls, and
God—and declares it to be one, and with plenty of room
for plurality and differences. His *one* is a whole-of-many-
parts, but with no sharp distinctions, nothing abrupt. In
contrast to Zen and Advaita, no veil suddenly drops away
to reveal in a flash the "completely other." Instead, one can
work one's way up step-by-step from the lower regions of
ignorance to the proximity of God, guided by his grace.
Still, something like suspicion sometimes mingles with our
admiration for this perhaps all-too-coherent, all-too-
perfect system. It lacks the igniting spark we find with
Shankara. What is missing is the ultimate explosion which
brings down the entire maya-edifice along with the celestial
realms—and propels us into a non-duality beyond words.

This is not to say that Ramanuja's system is somehow
"wrong." His perspective is perfectly legitimate. It is also
not so much "a preliminary stage to Shankara's ultimate
truth" (the phrasing preferred by many modern followers
of Vedanta), as a *subsequent* stage, or at least one that both
precedes and follows it. Anyone who breaks out of the
organic whole—the *one*—and experiences the "completely
other," may, as did Ramanuja, subsequently delight again
in the one-and-the-many, in God's omnipresence—only
this time with thoroughly purified eyes. Unfortunately, very

few ever reach this synthesis and express it in their lives—
one reason why the history of religion is so often only a
wholly unnecessary series of polemics.

Like Shankara, Ramanuja, also, was not one of those
enlightened sages who took to roaming the world like in-
toxicated mendicants. Much as Ramanuja played off love
of the personal god against Shankara's Advaita, his bhakti
remained rather moderate—particularly when measured
by the frenzy of a Chaitanya—and often even became fro-
zen in the formal aspects of his religion, something perhaps
common to all systematizers. Ramanuja still held fast to
tradition. In all fairness it must be said in this connection,
however, that he, and all those who succeeded him in
preaching personal love of God, made the barriers between
castes and between men and women much more permeable
than did Shankara. Shankara never applied his more intellectual Advaita in any radical way to social considerations.
It is not exactly to his credit that he translated so little of his
teaching of not-twoness and non-discrimination into actual
practice. In this respect his enlightened jnana-eye remained
blind. He kept strictly to the rigid rules of Hindu orthodoxy. The social barriers were of course not suddenly broken down by the bhakta, but members of the lower castes
and women came to have a better chance of becoming
involved in the bhakti-movements than in the much more
elitist circles of Advaita Vedanta.

Ramanuja's work and that of other founders of more
philosophical bhakti-schools does, however, present us
with a problem: to what extent is love of God compatible
with systematic thinking? We admire the ecstatic bhakti-
saint who in never-ending hymns celebrates the omniscience
of his god—and we also admire the jnani who slashes his

way to the absolute with the Sword of Differentiation. But problems arise when the bhakta also wants to be a jnani and in competition with him attempts to systematize his love of God.

DISTINCTION OR IDENTITY?

What we said above seems to apply particularly to Madhva (1199–1278). He distanced himself so far from Shankara's Advaita that he called his system Dvaita (two-ness, duality), the exact opposite of Shankara's. Madhva opposed the identity of God and the human soul but also broke with Ramanuja's organic unity of God and the world. To Madhva, each soul is different from every other soul, and each is totally distinct from God. The gulf between creator and Creation is almost as wide as it is in the strictly monotheistic religions of Judaism and Islam. Because Madhva strongly emphasized divine grace and divided souls into categories of the elect and the damned, Madhva's system is reminiscent of the theology of Calvinism. He is the only Vedantin to proclaim that evil souls are predestined to eternal damnation. Since he also taught a kind of trinity— with God's son, the wind-god Vayu, as his "mediator" in the world—some detect Christian influences in his work. It seems more likely, however, that Madhva carried to extremes only certain tendencies already present in theistic Vedanta, tendencies we already find in the Gita. Here and there his system exerted considerable influence, especially on Bengali Vaishnavism. Yet Ramanuja's Vishisht-Advaita, which takes the middle path between the monistic and dualistic extremes, seems far more typical of the prevailing religious mood in India.

Besides the schools already mentioned, there were many others which tried to explain the relationship of the world and individual souls to Brahman, often in terms that sounded paradoxical. Some called themselves Bheda-Abheda, which means that they adopted difference along with identity. All—from Vallabha, Nimbarka, and others, to Chaitanya—were Vaishnavas, and as such practiced fervent devotion to God in the form of Krishna. In their schools the personal god had fully replaced the suprapersonal Brahman of the Upanishads. In some of these circles the Radha-cult flourished, with Radha, Krishna's legendary sweetheart, personifying the "positive" side of maya-prakriti. Tantric tendencies were beginning to make themselves felt.

Bhakti-fervor probably reached its greatest intensity in the movement of the Bengali saint Chaitanya (1485–1533), who exhorted his followers to keep chanting God's name continually in order to keep the bhakti-vibrations pulsing. (The Hare-Krishna movement in the West is a latter-day offshoot of this Bengali bhakti-movement—with certain fanatical traits, long ago present in India, often being turned into caricaturelike exaggerations there.) Chaitanya himself is sometimes referred to as the founder of a school of Vedanta; but he was probably too immersed in the spirit of bhakti, in fervent devotion to Krishna, to have had any desire or inclination to set up a philosophical system. Before his "call" he had been a highly learned pandit; but afterward he tossed all his books into the Ganges in favor of wandering around the country dancing and singing, like some kind of Bengali St. Francis. It was his disciples who worked out a "system." Since it is typical of a certain bhakti-trend in India, we shall briefly go into it here.

In some ways Shankara's "hierarchy" is stood on its head in this school: the path, instead of leading through transcendence of the personal god to the impersonal absolute, leads through Nirguna Brahman to the innermost chamber of love where, in the very act of loving, the soul is one with the personal god—in this case Krishna. The attributeless, neutral Brahman is not denied but considered beyond the limits of human thought. As sheer being it permeates, supports, and "surrounds" the Lord Krishna. The devotee may feel the "undertow" of this limitless sea of Brahman, but the goal of his religious practice, rather than merging with the stream of sheer being, is to emerge from it purified and ready for wholly selfless worship of the Lord Krishna. The bhakta does not deny that a certain freedom from the bonds of prakriti is achievable, but he is not interested in the status of the jivanmukta, the liberated one, because it does not promote love of God. To followers of the bhakti-school, *mukti* (salvation, release) and *bhakti* (loving surrender) are inseparable. Bhakti's sole goal is more bhakti, ever greater love of God. It must be like the love of a lover who is free from any motive other than the very act of loving. To a bhakta this kind of love *is* the highest bliss.

A brief glance at Western mysticism may be in order here to help us understand these fine distinctions. We could think of Shankara's position as being represented there by (the "jnani and Advaitin") Meister Eckhart. He also held only the bare, completely "di-vested" *one* to be the ultimate reality. Just as Shankara distinguished between a higher (Nirguna) and a lower (Saguna) Brahman, so Eckhart distinguished between a supra-personal "Divine," the nameless ground (which he also sometimes called "Not-God"), and the personal "God," insofar as he is still worshiped as a person, as Father, Son, and Holy Ghost.

Most Christian theologians deny that there is such a "ground" behind or beyond the personal god. Yet there have also been mystics who did indeed acknowledge it, only they did not attach the same significance to it as Eckhart. These Christian mystics conceived of this ground more as pure being, something like an impersonal "essence" which the individual soul has in common with God and in which it is possible for the soul to immerse itself. But these mystics did not look on this immersion as the ultimate goal but rather as a transitional stage, a kind of bath in original being in preparation for the soul's encounter with God.

How to decide this conflict, as regards the West as well as India? One thing at least seems certain: both the advocates of a personal god and the advocates of an impersonal god are doubtless too hasty in their judgment of each other. There are those who look down on belief in a personal god and brush it aside as so-called "popular piety," when they themselves have never encountered God. And there are those who magnanimously grant preliminary and transitional status to the impersonal "ground of pure being," when they themselves have never come close to, let alone experienced, total immersion. In both cases we are up against misunderstandings. Thus the personal god is often regarded as mere "projection," devoid of objective reality, a view forgetful of the fact that as long as the "I" is experienced as real, the "Thou" of God must be real as well. As long as "I" believe in Creation, "I" must perforce believe in a creator. At this relative level, even Shankara admitted the personal god. The way he saw it: God can be transcended only when everything else is transcended, above all the human "I." No self can ever transcend God because before it could do so it would have to die as a separate self. Relinquishing the self is a precondition to immersion in Brahman. When this happens, the effect vanishes along with the cause, the creature along with the creator. The *one* is all that remains.

Theists, on the other hand, tend to regard this *one,* or ground, as merely a substratum or a kind of environment. One suspects that it is often confused with unmanifest prakriti, with the womb of Nature which brings forth all forms but is itself formless. From the point of view of the jnani, however, Nirguna Brahman is not an ocean surrounding Krishna, or some kind of mantle, or a diffuse, nebulous aura. Instead, Nirguna Brahman is simply pure and unadorned divinity, what remains when Krishna is divested of all that surrounds him, all embellishments. The jnani considered Nirguna not just as one more of God's attributes, but as the absence of any and all attributes.

But many a jnani must ask himself whether in holding love to be at best a way and means to an end, he is not perhaps really bypassing the true nature of love. The claim that love is absolute is fully justified. Truly selfless love is equal to attainment precisely because it is beyond all desire to attain. Is this kind of bhakta-saint so very different from the "mad" sage—the subject of so much praise in Advaita texts—who has also extinguished all desire to attain anything? Is not the divine the source of both loving surrender *and* highest knowledge—before a distinction was made between them? And do such distinctions not belong to the world of maya, the same world where the jnana-schools and bhakti-schools also are locked in endless, and largely loveless, debate as to which of the two leads deeper into the heart of the divine?

The weakness of many Indian bhakti-cults—when compared to Western versions of theism—is perhaps their tendency to see the person of God too much as a well-defined figure. Their iconography is fixed down to the minutest detail. Of course, this concreteness, this touchable presence of God—as long as it is understood as being only something provisional—can be helpful. But when this conception also becomes the basis for a theological-philosophical system where this clearly defined "God," with all the insignia of his might, is supposed to transcend even Nirguna Brahman, then we are clearly on sectarian grounds, outside the realm of serious philosophy. It was absolutely legitimate and necessary to criticize Shankara's one-sidedness and to defend the Citadel of God. But one can not defeat Shankara's Advaita by declaring that his pure absolute in truth wears yellow robes and is adorned with a peacock feather!

The Return of Shakti: God's Creative Power

BETWEEN OUR LATE Middle Ages and the nineteenth century, no other important Vedanta schools developed in India. Philosophically this period was unproductive and merely one in which the already established schools ruminated endlessly on the knowledge they had already gained. Of course, even this period had its prominent saints and through contact with Islam and Tantric influences all kinds of regroupings did take place, but the "classical" Vedanta schools were not much affected by all this.

RAMAKRISHNA: SON OF THE DIVINE MOTHER

Only around the middle and toward the end of the nineteenth century did things begin to stir again in this otherwise fallow field. The most significant and colorful figure of the time was undoubtedly Shri Ramakrishna (1836–1886). With him began the so-called Hindu Renaissance, the effects of which were soon felt in the West as well.

Ramakrishna was not actually a philosopher in the strict sense of the word, nor was he an acharya who would found a new school. He wrote no commentary on the sacred scriptures—indeed he could barely write. If we must label him at all, he would at first seem to fit in best with the theistic Vedanta schools, somewhere between Ramanuja and Chaitanya. (In his fervent love of God, Ramakrishna so much resembled Chaitanya that many celebrated him as a reincarnation of the latter.)

Yet Ramakrishna's greatness consisted precisely in his paying little attention to established categories; he could not be pigeonholed. There is no doubt that he was a great bhakta, filled with love for the personal god, but he favored worshiping him in the form of Shakti, the Divine Mother. This strongly Tantric overtone placed him outside the framework of classical Vedantic theism, its cults being confined almost exclusively to the worship of Vishnu and Krishna. He also accepted a follower of Advaita-Vedanta, Totapuri, as his guru. It was under his spiritual guidance that he experienced nirvikalpa samadhi (the state where all distinctions between God and the individual soul disappear) and had himself initiated as a monk of the Shankara order. (The Ramakrishna order, later established by his disciple Vivekananda, also clearly follows the Shankara tradition, their publications keeping mainly to the Advaita line.)

Nevertheless, neither Ramakrishna nor his disciples can be claimed exclusively by the Shankara school. In him and through him a new spirit emerged which, while still availing itself of the language of the medieval Vedanta schools for the elucidation of this or that complex of problems, at the same time remained above the fray, as though a new freedom had suddenly opened up where the old differences no longer mattered very much.

With regard to Shankara, Ramakrishna shared his view that the various Hindu divinities should be regarded as equally valid aspects of the supra-personal Brahman; and although as a bhakta he was closest to the circles of the Vaishnavas, he often criticized the fanaticism of those among them who would tolerate only Vishnu or (especially) Krishna as the highest god. Shankara's "magnanimity" had in part been a kind of indifference: the reason he accepted the various deities as equally valid was because he saw the impersonal Nirguna Brahman as undifferentiated reality. Thus all these divinities were to him mere shadows and it did not matter very much to him which of these a person happened to worship. Shankara had considered it much more important to transcend all these maya-shadows, enabling one to enter the clear light of the supra-personal.

Ramakrishna himself had succeeded in entering this supra-personal "zone." Indeed, with the jnana—Sword of Discrimination which his Advaita guru Totapuri had pressed into his hand, he had cut off even the image of his beloved Divine Mother—root of all forms and personifications—enabling him to plunge into the ocean of absolute consciousness. But unlike Shankara he did not as a result of this experience call into question the reality of the personal god and "His" Creation. He quite simply looked on these as the *other* side of the absolute: the dynamic-creative and personal side, its life, so to speak. He did not look on the absolute as silent, unproductive space. He criticized the one-sidedness of his guru Totapuri, who sought salvation exclusively in a rigid monism which left no room for diversity, who was incapable of accepting a more flexible Advaita that would include Shakti and her Creation. Why this one-sidedness? Why only the static, the formless, and the impersonal? Why not also the overflowing abundance of his Divine Mother? Ramakrishna often said that he did not want to play just *one* note on his flute but wanted to elicit from it all possible notes. "Why lead a monotonous life? I like to prepare fish in a variety of ways: sometimes curried, sometimes fried, sometimes pickled, and so forth. Sometimes I worship God by ritual, sometimes by repeating His name, sometimes by meditation, sometimes in song and sometimes in dance."[15]

In Ramakrishna's case, all aspects of the divine reality were equally valid, not because of indifference but because his intense love embraced them all—including even Christ and the God of Islam. He did not just "tolerate" them. Quite the contrary! He *lived* with them, became totally absorbed in them, and in turn discovered each to be a gateway to the impersonal absolute, in his eyes their common ground.

We never have the impression that Ramakrishna consciously labored to achieve this synthesis of the different religious traditions; he quite simply experienced them without the slightest sectarian prejudice, then in the end declared that each revealed a certain aspect of the divine reality. He compared God to a chameleon which constantly changes color, saying that people get into arguments about it because each has seen the chameleon only briefly and one asserts that it is a beautiful red, the other that it is a bright green; that only the one actually living under the tree where the chameleon also lives knows that it takes on different colors—even sometimes seeming to be without any color at all.[16] "God has many names and innumerable forms, through which we can approach Him. . . . Just as water is called by different names in various languages—one calling it 'water,' another 'vari,' a third 'aqua,' and a fourth 'pani'—so is the one Sat-chit-ananda called by some 'God,' by others 'Allah,' by some 'Hari,' and again by others 'Brahman.' "[17] With respect to the different religions, the oneness in all this multiplicity was so obvious to him that keeping each in a separate compartment did not even occur to him. That is why when we first read him he appears to be saying one thing alongside another. We find Advaita wisdom right alongside soul-melting love of God, elaborations on the impersonal nature of Brahman alongside words concerning the Divine Mother or the mystery of divine incarnation.

Friendly and peaceable as Ramakrishna usually was, he would clearly get angry when someone refused to accept Shakti, "his" Divine Mother (whom he also worshiped as Kali), for instance, in the name of a strict monism: "Kali is verily Brahman, and Brahman is verily Kali. It is one and the same Reality. When we think of It as inactive, that is to say, not engaged in acts of creation, preservation, and destruction, then we call It Brahman. But when It engages in these activities, then we call It Kali or Shakti. The Reality is one and the same; the difference is in name and form." He insisted that, "My Divine Mother is none other than the Brahman. . . ."[18] "Brahman and Shakti are identical. If you accept the one, you must accept the other. It is like fire and its power to burn. If you see the fire, you must recognize its power to burn also. You cannot think of the power to burn without fire. You cannot conceive of the sun's rays without the sun, nor can you conceive of the sun without rays. . . ." Ramakrishna never tired of explaining the relation between the formless absolute and the personal god with his Shakti, his divine power. "What is milk like? Oh, you say, it is something white. You cannot think of milk without whiteness, and again, you cannot think of whiteness without milk. Thus you cannot think of Brahman without Shakti, or of Shakti without Brahman. One cannot think of the Absolute without the Relative, or of the Relative without the Absolute."[19]

Ramakrishna's conception of the identity of the impersonal Brahman and its Shakti, its personification as Mother of the Universe, resembles the Christian theological conception of the relation between the "hidden" Father and the revealed Logos, the Son, without whom nothing has come into being. Still, the spectrum in which the invisible divinity's effulgence is reflected is in the case of Ramakrishna's Shakti more colorful, perhaps, than it is in the Christian Logos, where all "darker" sides are excluded.

It is true that Ramakrishna acknowledged a reality beyond the domain of Shakti: the very Nirguna Brahman, the undifferentiated consciousness he had himself experienced in deepest samadhi. Explaining this he said, "But though you reason all your life, unless you are established in samadhi, you cannot go beyond the jurisdiction of Shakti. . . ."[20] And yet his experience did not cause him to give up Shakti worship. While, with Shankara, only a denial of maya's creative powers led to not-twoness or Advaita, with Ramakrishna it was precisely the vision of the inseparable oneness of the absolute and the relative that constituted *true* Advaita.

In a sense Ramakrishna recaptured the original spirit of the Upanishads where such sharp distinctions between a higher and a lower Brahman, as Shankara had made them, did not yet exist. Of course, he did not really use the language of the Upanishads; in fact, he seldom quoted from them at all. He seemed much more at home in the world of the popular tales, the Puranas. After having absorbed the many versions of the various religio-philosophical ideas since the age of the Upanishads he simply combined and lived them. The result was a very flexible Advaita where, rather than Brahman's static aspect being the dominant one, Brahman's creative expansion came into focus again—only now, under Tantric influence, this creative power attained the status of an independent divinity as Shakti or Divine Mother. Her positively conceived creative power had now replaced the more negatively conceived maya of Shankara and of Sankhya's prakriti. Ramakrishna often stressed that only he is in possession of the whole truth who does not remain in the no-man's-land of the impersonal Brahman but returns to view all there is as Brahman—only this time with eyes open.

After Shankara's radical maya-teaching had made a roughly pantheistic misinterpretation impossible (although this, in turn, led to the danger of an equally radical acosmism to immediately appear on the horizon) the time had now come, perhaps, for inclusion of the role of the divine in the world. When Ramakrishna keeps saying that God has "become" the world, a knowledgeable Advaitin might frown and hasten to add that this "having become all this" is in fact only something that *appears* to be so. But of what use is this sort of intellectual argumentation in the face of a direct insight which floods everything with divine light? Ramakrishna had not seen a mirage, he had experienced the Brahman-as-Creation very concretely—and as something sacred. His experience thus linked up again with the fundamental insights of the Vedic seers, insights which seemed to have been lost in the intellectualized atmosphere of many Advaita schools.

Ramakrishna saw maya as being of two kinds. He said that *avidya-maya* (the maya of ignorance) deludes, but that *vidya-maya* (the maya of wisdom) "begets devotion, kindness, wisdom and love, which leads to God. Avidya must be propitiated, and that is the purpose of the rites of Shakti worship."[21] But he also stressed how much "his" Mother was in love with the play of the gunas, with the Cosmic Dance (*lila*): "The Divine Mother is always sportive and playful. The whole universe is Her play."[22] She is Brahman's "being-beside-itself," its outer appearance. Both aspects, the dark and the light, are now reconciled.

Here at last is the "bite" we missed with Ramajuna and most theistic Vedanta schools, which saw in God only a paragon of positive virtues. The well-rounded, somewhat overly simplistic character of their theism came to be shattered by Ramakrishna, not only because of the reintroduction of Nirguna, "the altogether different," but also because of the Tantric conception of Shakti as the totality of all there is. Shankara's one-sidedness could be overcome only at this appropriately high level and his transcendence still be transcended. "The altogether different," the Nirguna Brahman, is reflected again, so to speak, in the mysteriously paradoxical Shakti—and both were now fully accepted. Ramakrishna saw in Nirguna Brahman, in emptiness, the face of his Divine Mother who, outwardly, "expressed" absolute emptiness through absolute fullness.

When we study Ramakrishna's sayings and delve deeply into the life of this great Indian mystic—whom his disciples venerated as an avatar or divine incarnation—many of the

scholastic disputes of medieval Vedanta seem quite insub-
stantial. One even hesitates to label Ramakrishna a Vedantin, to saddle a religious genius like him with the name of a
school. In an atmosphere where only direct experience
counts such labels become meaningless—were the rishis of
the Upanishads "Vedantins"?—and when such names take
on a more or less fixed meaning, they also take on ideological overtones. Although indeed an Advaita-Vedantin, as
well as a Vaishnava devoted to Krishna, and also a Tantric,
he was also much more than these labels imply. He himself
used the word *Vedanta* mainly to refer to Shankara's
school, frequently criticizing its one-sidedness; indeed he
prayed to the Divine Mother not to let him become a "dry
jnani." He reproached the Vedantins of the Shankara line
with not accepting divine incarnation, or holding it at least
to be non-essential. And when on his deathbed he said to
his disciple Vivekananda, "He who was Rama and
Krishna, in this body now is Ramakrishna," he added, "but
not in your Vedantic sense!" He did not want to see lost in
the Advaita perspective what was "special" about divine
incarnation, swallowed up, as it were, in a view where
every human being—indeed every speck of dust—was simply one with Brahman.

It must not be forgotten, however, that Ramakrishna
himself nudged his disciples toward Advaita. At times, he
had Vivekananda read to him from the radical Ashtavakra
Samhita, and when Vivekananda would vigorously protest
against the idea that, ultimately, there was indeed only the
one Brahman and refused to continue reading from this
"atheistic" scripture, Ramakrishna would only smile. He
was well acquainted with his disciple's strong Shiva nature.
Soon Vivekananda would himself experience non-duality:

positively, by suddenly seeing to his astonishment that all is Brahman and that the world of appearances—including his own existence—is divine; and, negatively, by being hurled into the depth of nirvikalpa samadhi, into this transcendental black hole, which gulped up everything, even himself.

VIVEKANANDA: YOU ARE GODS!

Swami Vivekananda (1863–1902) was to become a passionate herald of Advaita-Vedanta who spread the universal message of his master Ramakrishna both in India and the West. As we already indicated in the introduction, in America and Europe he used the term Vedanta for the "purified" version of Hinduism he presented to his audiences, a version purged of local myth and legend. But even in India he increasingly used the name Vedanta—clearly as a unifying term of the many variant schools—as when referring to it as an extensive step-by-step structure where everything has its place, both individual worship of the personal god and the experience of the impersonal Brahman. Somewhat simplified, we might say that Vivekananda taught Shankara's Advaita-Vedanta, enriched by the all-inclusive experiences of his master Ramakrishna—experiences which also allowed for more of the devotional bhakti-aspect, not only of Hinduism, but also of Christianity and Islam. Vivekananda often said that in Ramakrishna the intellect of Shankara and the heart of Chaitanya had come together. Like his master, Vivekananda worshiped Shakti, the Divine Mother, but called this a personal preference. And like him, he also did not sweep aside the world of maya as radically as Shankara had done but accepted the relative as the dynamic aspect of the absolute.

Vivekananda believed he could bring together under one umbrella the various Vedanta schools—Shankara's pure Advaita, Ramanuja's qualified non-dualism, and Madhva's dualism, and even the theological systems of other religions—by arranging them as stages one above the other. Ramakrishna himself had often suggested this idea, for instance when he quoted Hanuman's words from the Puranas: "O Rama, sometimes I worship You as the One, as Absolute Abundance. Then I look upon myself as a part of You. Sometimes I meditate on You, O Rama, as my Divine Lord. Then I look upon myself as Your servant. But when, O Rama, I am graced with the highest Knowledge, I see and know that I am You and You are me." Yet it was typical of Ramakrishna that he never gave these ideas any hierarchical structure by ranking one above the other. Vivekananda, on the other hand—appearing as he did before more philosophically trained and interested audiences—had to bring a bit more order to these different religious experiences. It seemed appropriate to him to begin with a simple dualism, at the lowest level so to speak, where man regards himself as God's creature and sees in him an all-powerful fatherly ruler, and to end with oneness at the highest level where man, completely emancipated, has integrated the various representations of divinity and discovered that he himself is Atman, the divine Self. Of course, this kind of ranking still showed traces of Shankara's influence and could hardly be regarded as a synthesis by, say, a follower of Madhva, still less by a Christian, Moslem, or Jew, insofar as each regarded the gulf between Creator and creature as unbridgeable. How could any of them be grateful to Vivekananda for having assigned them the lowest level? Especially in the West, however, this step-by-step approach to the absolute made sense to many who considered traditional theology outmoded. In almost all Vedanta groups in the West, as well as in those Indian circles particularly oriented toward Vivekananda and the Ramakrishna order, this structure came to be accepted as a kind of universal Vedanta.

Vivekananda's teachings were basically variations on a single theme: that man's true nature or Self, the Atman, innately contains all within it. Man was seen as the slumbering god who, lulled to sleep by maya, dreams away one lifetime after another until, one day, he wakes up and shakes off the superstitious view that he is only a wretched creature created out of nothing by a tyrannical god. "Gradually this giant awakens and, conscious of his infinite dimensions, rouses himself."[23] "What the sages have been searching for everywhere is in our own hearts. . . . The freedom you perceived was indeed there, but you projected it outside yourself, and that was your mistake. Bring it nearer and nearer, until you find that it was all the time within you. It is the Self of your own self. That freedom is your own nature, and maya has never bound you. Nature never has power over you. Like frightened children you were dreaming that it was throttling you, and the release from this fear is the goal. It is not enough to grasp this only with your mind. It is necessary that you see it directly, actualize it—much more directly than we perceive this world here. Then we shall know that we are free. Then, and then alone, will all difficulties disappear, will all the perplexities of the heart be smoothed away, all that is crooked become straight, will the delusion of multiplicity in Nature be dissolved and maya, instead of being the terrifying, hopeless dream that it is now, will change into something beautiful, and this world, instead of being a prison, will be your playing field; even dangers and difficulties, even all sufferings, will be seen in a divine light, will reveal their true nature and show us that He is behind everything, as the true substance of everything, and that He alone is the one true Self."[24]

Vivekananda stressed the realization of oneness so much because only it can drive away the specters of fear and weakness. As soon as we think of ourselves as isolated beings, fear is there along with the feeling that we are weak and helpless. Vivekananda took up again one of the key words of the Upanishads: the *infinite*. "It is I who am eating with a million mouths. How could I be hungry? It is I who am working with innumerable hands. How could I be inactive? It is I who am living the life of the whole universe. How could there be death? I am beyond life and death. Why seek release? I am by nature free. What could fetter me, the Lord of the Universe? The sacred texts of the world are but small sketches attempting to describe my greatness—this infinite dimension of mine. I am the universe's sole existence. Of what significance these books . . . When man has recognized himself as one with the Infinite, when all separateness has disappeared, when all men and women, all gods and angels, all animals and plants, when the entire universe has become that Oneness, then there is no fear. Can I injure my Self? Can I kill my Self? Who is there to fear? Can I fear my Self? . . ."[25]

Vivekananda did not, however, confine himself to such clarion calls, such flights of the spirit; he was also and above all concerned with putting Vedanta into *practice*, making it relevant to everyday life. "We must be able to apply it to every aspect of our lives. But not only this. The erroneous differentiation between religion and life-in-this-

world must go. Vedanta teaches Oneness, one life throughout."[26] He called it a scandal that in the very country that
gave birth to Advaita there were so many barriers in the
people's daily lives; and he did not hesitate to reproach
Shankara with orthodox narrow-mindedness in the social
realm. In his view, Atman consciousness should fill every
man and woman with pride irrespective of gender and
caste; through this knowledge of unity the old maya-
barriers would then gradually disappear. His ideal was that
of the universal man living fully in this oneness and at the
same time having the strength to be actively engaged in this
relative world.

He never understood this active commitment as "help-
ing." He always understood it as "serving," serving the one
God manifest in everyone, not least in the weak, the sick,
the meek, and the helpless. To this end he founded and
organized the Ramakrishna order. The monks of this order
do not conceive of their status as monk-sannyasins as
merely meaning freedom *from* something—such as freedom from the bonds of nature and society—but also as
conferring upon them the freedom to serve their fellow
men. This was shocking to the orthodoxy, to those who
associated monasticism only with a purely contemplative
life, and they reproached him with introducing Western
ideas. The question as to what extent Vivekananda may
have been influenced by Christian and humanistic ideals
cannot be pursued fully here, but one might argue that an
admission of such influence would hardly detract from his
greatness. A man striving for such perfect universality as he
did loses nothing by opening himself to the inspiration of
traditions other than his own. A certain national pride has
always insisted that all these "innovations" ultimately have

their roots exclusively in Indian soil; but this obsession with attributing everything to purely Indian traditions goes completely against the spirit of universality which India so audibly claims as her own.

At all events, through Vivekananda, Vedanta took on a form, both in its philosophical and its practical aspects, with which many Westerners could identify, even if they were not necessarily prepared to work their way through all the Brahma Sutra commentaries or accept the hairsplitting caste rules. His simplification of Vedanta meant clarification and intensification and was not a sell-out. He did not speak *about* Vedanta. He created it anew and directly communicated its spirit of fearlessness, oneness, infiniteness, joy, and fulfillment. He also wrested it from chauvinistic narrowness and merged it with the spiritual breath of all great mystic traditions—not least of all Johannine Christianity, *the* religion of the spirit.

If we must sort out the "contents" of his Vedanta, they are, greatly simplified, as follows: all Creation is the outward expression of Brahman, the creative potency of which continually generates new forms. In this process every being is destined to eventually rediscover his original true nature, even if only perhaps after thousands of lifetimes. Every soul is potentially divine. The purpose of life is to *manifest* this divine nature, whether it be by raja-yoga, the Path of Meditation (and control of the mind); by bhakti-yoga, the Path of Loving Devotion; by karma-yoga, the Path of Selfless Action (and service); or by jnana-yoga, the Path of Knowledge. In order that his life be as universal as possible—that it be the most perfect reflection of the abundance of the absolute—it is best to live by all these paths.

With regard to his special emphasis on karma-yoga, he could, of course, point to the Gita and other authoritative texts where the Path of Selfless Action had already been suggested. Yet Vivekananda had a much more positive motivation for such personal commitment to offer modern people than had, for instance, the Gita—with its only concrete motif being praise for a soldier's selfless commitment in war. For Vivekananda this sort of commitment was no longer foremost, combative as he himself often seemed to be. He kept using such metaphors as *physician* or *teacher*, people who are working toward a better world. He may well have found it quite absurd that many followers of Vedanta approved of the Gita's call to battle and the destructive actions of the soldier while tending to be suspicious of every positive action aimed at improving society. Vivekananda had enough of the spirit of Shiva in him to understand both: the ideal of the warrior-samurai, *and* the ideal of the monk-sannyasin who withdraws from the world. He probably saw the subtle connection between the two. For this reason, however, he may also have felt that what both were lacking was love and affirmation of life in this world, without which a really positive commitment is not possible.

Vivekananda's own affirmation was not always loud and clear, nor was it constant. Periods of strong social engagement repeatedly gave way to "otherworldly" moods when the physical world, with its many economic and social problems, seemed not to exist for him at all. One moment he speaks of a new Golden Age, the next he proclaims that there could never be an objective paradise, that there is only the subjective heavenly kingdom in the heart of the enlightened sage who everywhere sees only the Brahman. Because he almost always spoke spontaneously, one finds many seeming contradictions in his work. This makes him seem complicated—but also very much alive. When we keep in mind the many contradictory currents that must have clashed in him, it seems astonishing that anything quite so clear ever emerged. In his utterances, West and East— today's humanistic active engagement and a thousand-year-old ascetic tradition—came together. We should be grateful to the swami because, rather than giving us a refined version of the old Vedanta from a Himalayan cave, he actually *lived* this Vedanta in his short, stormy life and, putting it to the test, as it were, also put it on its feet—all the while holding fast to transcendence as well. In spite of his many otherworldly excursions, Vedanta began for him with seeing the divine Brahman in one's own fellow men— and that is also where it ended.

He promoted Advaita not least of all because this teaching seemed to him to offer a chance of bringing into focus what all these different religious traditions had in common. As long as these religions were characterized by dualism, as long as they created a gulf between Creator and created and fanatically held fast to whatever their own image of God, regarding all others of the devil, there could be no question of unity. Like Ramakrishna, Vivekananda was not interested in artificially creating a uniform religion, but he did work toward an end where all religions— including their own sectarian trends—would look on one another as so many paths to the same goal. The end of all these approaches could not possibly be a specific person with a specific name, but could only be supra-personal divine reality revealing itself in *all* deities, incarnations, prophets, and saints, the same reality with which all humans were also fundamentally one. According to Vivekananda and Vedanta in general, man—and with him the whole universe—is not "created" in the strict sense of the word and able, at best, to come nearer to God through Divine Grace—but *is* the divine, which through its own maya becomes seemingly finite and manifest as this or that particular individual.

This is why when addressing his audiences Vivekananda exclaimed again and again: "You are all gods!" This, the point of all his talks, was for many among them quite a challenge. And when he said that Hinduism should be more "aggressive"—as aggressive as Christianity and Islam—he did not mean that it should be about gods and goddesses, of course. He was seeking to put more emphasis on Vedanta's universal message of the "unknown god dormant in each individual"—so often prevented from awakening by "religious" teachings about sinfulness and an evil world. "Do not speak of the wickedness of the world and all its sins. Deplore that you still see wickedness at all. Deplore that you see sin everywhere. If you want to help the world, do not condemn it. Do not weaken it more. For what are sin and misery but results of weakness. The world is made weaker and weaker every day by such teachings. Men are taught from childhood that they are weak and sinful. Teach them that they are all wonderful children of immortality, even those who are still its weakest manifestations. . . ."[27]

Shortly before his untimely death, this compassionate monk, whose mind so often withdrew to the uninhabited heights of the snow-capped Himalayas, so to speak, only to come down again and again into the valleys where ordinary humans dwell, wrote: "I may be about to leave this body, slip it off like a worn-out garment; but I shall not cease to work! I shall continue to inspire people everywhere—until the world knows that it is one with God."

AUROBINDO: SHAKTI AS CREATIVE ENERGY

The return of Shakti, the creative power of the absolute, celebrated its greatest triumph in the figure of Shri Aurobindo (1872–1950). Like Ramakrishna and Vivekananda he was a native of Bengal. After studying in England, he initially belonged to a circle of revolutionary patriots who, not entirely by chance, looked on their "motherland" India as a manifestation of Shakti. Aurobindo at first used yoga techniques only as an aid to concentration while carrying on his political activities, but by and by yoga took possession of him, until a series of intense experiences in Alipur prison convinced him that he had to continue his work on a different plane. In Pondicherry a group of disciples soon began to form around him and his companion Mira Richards (henceforth to be known only as "the Mother"). When he died—or "withdrew"—in 1950, the once small original ashram had long since grown into an immense center of spiritual energy and become a whole "town."

Like Ramakrishna, Aurobindo was not a pure Vedantin, at least not in the mold of Shankara. In sharp contrast to this tradition and the classical yoga of Patanjali he was not so much concerned with release from the gross and subtle sheaths of individual existence—and to drop out of the game of life through absorption in an impersonal nirvana or Nirguna Brahman—as with becoming completely receptive to the divine energy, "to invite it down," so to speak, so that it might transform these physical and mental sheaths into perfect instruments of its omnipotence. Aurobindo did not deny that the realization of the transcendent impersonal Brahman nature in nirvikalpa samadhi was a provisional high point in human spiritual evolution. He

defended himself against the mistaken idea that he dis-
dained this spiritual tradition which had found such perfect
expression in Buddhism and Shankara's Mayavada. Responding to a remark by one of his students, he wrote,
somewhat sarcastically: "Wonderful! The realization of the
Self, which at the same time is liberation from the ego;
being aware of the One-in-all; having completely overcome
universal not-knowing; continual concentration of the
mind on the Highest, the Infinite, the Eternal ... all this is
not worth the trouble, not worth recommending, 'not a
very difficult step!' Nothing new! ... Why should there be
something new? The aim of the spiritual quest is to discover
what is eternally true—not what is true in time. Where did
you get this strange idea about the old yoga system and
yogis? Is the wisdom of Vedanta and Tantrism really so
trivial and insignificant? Tell me, have the Sadhaks of *this*
ashram really realized the true Self? Are they really liberated Jivanmuktas, free from ego and ignorance? I said this
yoga is 'new' because it aims at integrating the Divine in the
life of this world—rather than solely aiming at the beyond,
at a supra-mental realization. But does this justify contempt
for spiritual realization, which is just as much the aim of
this yoga as it is the aim of any other yoga system?"[28]

Yet Aurobindo also did not deny that he considered the
earlier paths too negative and one-sided. In his eyes they
were shortcuts to the absolute, ways that left the world and
humanity behind unchanged. Even Vivekananda—who
was comparatively more strongly influenced by Shankara's
Advaita—had stressed more of an evolutionary process in
some of his thinking. But what surfaced only sporadically
with Vivekananda became with Aurobindo the very heart
of an extensive and coherent system. He saw Brahman's
manifest Creation not as an illusion or empty play, but as

the gradual ascent of the divine from inert and unknowing gross physical matter toward perfect, divine consciousness—an ascent simultaneous with a "descent" of transcendent reality.

Actually, the idea of this sort of evolutionary ascent was not entirely alien to Indian thinking—even Shankara had seen in the play of maya a teleological arrow pointing from plant and animal existence to human awareness—which in turn furnished the basis, the very possibility, for enlightenment. But the focus had always been on the individual freeing himself from the wheel of life-and-death, which itself would, of course, eternally continue to revolve. Aurobindo on the other hand concentrated more on mundane consciousness and mankind as such. This is not to say that he thought it possible for all humanity to suddenly attain a state of perfection; but he did have in mind larger centers where the higher consciousness would become fully manifest; indeed he did not hesitate to speak of a new "race," an elite which in the interest of this higher evolution would be completely at the disposal of this higher divine power—not forgetting, of course, to sharply distinguish this new type of "superman" from Nietzschean ideas. He was striving for a new quality of life: the Brahman should not only be experienced at the spiritual summit by man as an oasis of silence and peace, but it should also *energize* human life with its creative potency, invigorate and enrich it in a world where life was so often barren. Life would then truly deserve to be called LIFE. Shakti's creative "imaginativeness" was, after all, not exhausted, its evolutionary play (lila) was not over. The whole point could not be solely the creation of a few tiny isolated islands of enlightenment here and there in a sea of ignorance. The divine was to be attained and realized by man not only at the "climax of the soul," but the *whole* man, the *whole* earth was to be the receptacle of divine consciousness and its dynamic energy. Aurobindo did not believe in casting off the sheaths of the Atman like useless parts, but in transforming them. He saw the fully realized man not as someone enlightened only in the upper strata of his being, but as one transformed by the energy of the divine, right down to the last cell of his body.

Some of this reminds one of Christian ideas like the Resurrection, which involves the body as well; or the "new heaven on earth." But Aurobindo sought his roots also in Indian, especially Vedic, tradition. We see this in something he wrote in an early letter to "the Mother": "We have conquered heaven, but not the earth; yet the perfection of yoga consists, as the Vedas say, in 'uniting heaven and earth.' "29

Other things in Aurobindo's work have an occult Gnostic ring. It is probably mainly this feature that puts off some "pure" Vedantins and keeps them from surrendering to the world of Aurobindo. But although Aurobindo put strong emphasis on the personal god, the Purushottama of the Gita, and never concealed his aversion to an impersonal monism, even the bhaktas have a hard time with him. For while a bhakta has in his head, and especially in his heart, nothing but pure love of God—to whom he surrenders everything, including all thought of the future and the social transformation of this world—there is a certain Faustian trait in Aurobindo, a great aspiration, an "experimenting from below," so to speak. Typically, he said of Ramakrishna that, with all his greatness, he had only known pure love of his Divine Mother, nothing else. In a way he is right: Ramakrishna left all plans for improving the world to his Divine Mother. Still, one might ask what could prevent her from creating in Aurobindo and his

Shakti (the Mother of the ashram) a new bridgehead here on earth and through them preparing for a new stage in evolution? What does it mean, after all, to leave everything to God? Assuming He were interested in raising life in this world to a new level, would He not need as his medium human beings who were completely receptive to His higher power? Viewed "from below," many a human endeavor might look like Faustian striving, mere human exertion, while what it would really be all about would be the struggle of divine consciousness with the sluggishness of the coarser sheaths.

How tough this work really was became particularly apparent when Aurobindo endeavored to suffuse even the consciousness of the bodily cells with divine light. The resistance was tremendous. In the end he probably did not achieve much more in this regard than so many great yogis before him—namely the ability to leave the body consciously and serenely when his earthly mission is for the time fulfilled.

Yet even for the critically inclined observer there is no question that we are dealing in Pondicherry—as in other projects such as Auroville—with one of the greatest and most forward-looking adventures in this century. The impulse Aurobindo gave to India can hardly be overestimated: the emphasis on evolution, history, the person, and the community—together an extremely important counterpoint to the purely individualistic salvation-teaching of classical Vedanta. Vivekananda had already sensed that many Indians lacked positive motivation. "This idea of Satya-Yuga [Golden Age] is what will really reinvigorate India, believe me," he wrote in a letter.[30] In Aurobindo's work we have a perspective which knows not only a perfectly immutable absolute—besides an empty idling in maya—but also a vision of the conscious transformation of the world, its banner emblazoned with hope. This is a vision which also appeals to young Westerners looking for motivating guidance on how to act. Classical karma-yoga, as taught in the Gita, is actually only about the fulfillment of duty—a kind of action for action's sake—a way of purification which ultimately brings release from what was perceived, after all, as a vale of tears. Such karma-yoga required skill and extreme concentration as well as perseverance and humility, but not really much creativity. It does not seek to restructure and transform anything, but only to ensure that the wheel of life is kept turning—and that the one involved, once purified by this selfless action, is at last freed from this wheel.

Perhaps some products of this newly awakened creativity look to us a little quaint now; but we have to admit that something was set in motion here which makes the earlier alternatives of withdrawal from or commitment to the world seem quite outdated. The mere "spiritualists" were not interested in transforming the world and those committed to it were not able to transform it—at least not in a positive sense—because they were still acting at the ego-level and often only made things worse. But the point now was to combine progressive, creative action with transformation of consciousness, which begins with opening up and stepping aside in order to become receptive to spiritual strength "from above." The supra-mental reality, regarded by Aurobindo as the ultimate aim, transcended the earlier antithesis of static immobility versus creatively productive activity and was thus closer to the Brahman of the Upanishads than to the strongly ideological absolute of Shankara.

That Aurobindo was by no means just a philosopher

influenced by the West, but is to be counted among the rishis, is clearly shown by his commentaries on several Upanishads, as well as a number of pre-Upanishadic texts, which often exhibit entirely new insights. He thus combined ancient Vedic intuitions with today's humanitarian expectations. The connecting link was precisely the positive spirit, the *yes* to this world, and with it, directly or indirectly, a rejection of a religion which renounced the world and which, although occupying a proper place in the spiritual evolution of man, could not claim to be the last word for all time.

RAMANA MAHARSHI: PURE BEING

Ramana Maharshi, the sage of Arunachala, who also died in 1950, appears to be the exact opposite of Shri Aurobindo. In his life and sayings we see little of a "return of Shakti." Spellbound and absorbed by an immutable absolute with no room for evolutionary development toward "a new earth," he still seems to belong entirely to the old Advaita school of Shankara.

Had Ramana Maharshi, however, been only one more representative of this school, he would hardly need mentioning here. There have always been, and there still are, enough representatives of the Shankara tradition in the twentieth century given to much wordier proclamations of this tradition and the Mayavada teaching than this rather taciturn sage. What made Ramana Maharshi so extraordinary was that he so clearly, directly, and uncompromisingly embodied the truth of this teaching (the same truth Aurobindo knew) that even those who could not live without active engagement in the world rarely failed to admire him. In the figure of this enlightened sage we are face to face with something irreducible: sheer and perfect being, unconcerned with the disputes among those holding different views. For many, one look into his eyes meant more than the study of all the Vedanta scriptures combined, including all of Shankara's commentaries. It was as if all that was not essential to this teaching had over the centuries been burned so that we could now be shown the naked truth in the person of this holy man. The medieval scholastic attire is gone once and for all, and we are astonished at how modern and contemporary eternal truth can be.

In Aurobindo and Ramana Maharshi we see two prototypes who, although differing sharply in many ways, are at the very least equal in stature. They represent, respectively, the static and the dynamic view of divine reality. In actual practice, certain dangers are obvious in both approaches: at the static-passive end, too much of a closed system involving a certain sterility, a perfection somehow negative and wanting; at the dynamic end, an overemphasis on the quest—one that never really aims at the ultimate—a constant becoming and Faustian striving that is itself elevated to the status of something absolute and sees beyond every peak only still farther distant peaks. Of course, Aurobindo himself can hardly be blamed for such romanticism. He was, after all, just as much at home in sheer being as Ramana Maharshi was; and anyone familiar with the life and sayings of Ramana Maharshi knows how open in all his perfection this sage could be. Although arrived and wanting nothing more, he did not give the impression of being dead to the world. Rather, he embodied in a much quieter way than Aurobindo the truth that being is also being alive. (Actually, Aurobindo also lived very much secluded during the last decade of his life, almost more withdrawn from public view than the "passive" sage Ramana—to say nothing of Ramakrishna, and especially Vivekananda.)

The story of Ramana's spiritual awakening is already part of the classical lore of modern Vedanta. Once, while his mind was intensely focused on dying, the apparently previously quite normal boy suddenly awakened to the reality of the Atman, the true Self—not to be confused with our limited mortal ego. After this realization, nothing could keep him at his parental home. He left, as he wrote in a note, "to look for the real father." Eventually arriving at the sacred mountain Arunachala, he spent the next five years in almost uninterrupted meditation. For a long time his pronouncements were extremely brief. We can hardly find anything resembling a "development" in his life. His awakening was sudden; it was not the result of any refined yoga method, and his later meditation was just a constant rootedness in the absolute. Ramana Maharshi alluded only to a progress from nirvikalpa samadhi to *sahaja samadhi*. He understood this as temporary immersion in absolute consciousness followed by normal everyday awareness. But over the years even this kind of immersion, this "disappearing" in the absolute, ceased, and sahaja samadhi remained his natural state, a state of awareness and spontaneity that governed all he did, whether he was speaking to someone or feeding a dog.

For many people in this century Ramana Maharshi thus became the epitome of the legendary Vedantic jivanmukta, "the one liberated in this body." Contributing still further to this reverence was the circumstance that no sensationalism surrounded this holy man. Seekers were not offered champagne here, but crystal-clear mountain spring water. The Advaita he embodied had lost its pedantic and somewhat cumbersome dogmatic trait. What remained was only the continually repeated question "Who am I?" which every visitor had to keep asking himself over and over again. Ramana avoided responding instantly to questions with the Vedantic clarion call: "You are Brahman, Infinite Being. . . ." To such assertions—almost ready-made answers—he preferred silence, a silence where the truth would have to emerge without words. A Ramana Maharshi may not motivate us to great deeds; but he is the mirror we now and then need if, in our willful activities, we want to avoid kidding ourselves. This, by the way, applies equally to those who have no use at all for reshaping and transforming the world, who wrap themselves in private piety and allow the silence of meditation to lull the mind. In this connection the Ramana quotation we introduced in the section on "Deep Sleep and Illumination" shows how unpleasantly revealing the sharp eye of this enlightened holy man can be for such people. His incorruptible eye is not so much concerned with detecting whether someone is leading an active or a contemplative life; but it does detect instantly when someone with the wrong attitude then also tries to defend it on ideological grounds. Almost anything can be used to serve in such a defense, even Vedanta.

Besides Shri Aurobindo and Ramana Maharshi there were and still are a great many yogis, holy men, scholars, and others, who have made a name for themselves in twentieth-century India and who, to a greater or lesser extent, also cite the Vedanta doctrines as their authority and have found a following in the West. We find eloquent philosophers like S. Radhakrishnan alongside silent sages; ardent and deeply humble bhaktas like Ram-Das alongside fashionable gurus whose well-organized "lectures," although larded with quotations from the Upanishads, barely convey the spirit of these books. Besides the swamis of the Ramakrishna Mission, it was above all Paramahansa Yogananda and Swami Shivananda of Rishikesh, and their respective organizations, who ensured the dissemination of Vedanta philosophy to the West. For many pilgrims to India in search of an enlightened soul the great Ananda Mayi Ma became the focus of attraction; others found their guru in the miracle-worker Sai Baba. Maharishi Mahesh Yogi, who became so popular in the West, actually belongs to the traditional Shankara lineage; but when looking at the excesses of the organization one may sometimes wonder whether Shankara would have recognized himself in this meditation movement. In the case of others, such as Bhagvan Rajneesh, Vedanta is only one of many adornments in their outwardly uniform but intellectually multicolored array. The younger generation of the West cares little, in any case, about strict demarcations; for them Vedanta shades off into elements of Zen and Sufism, and Yoga methods mingle with Western therapy. This brings us to the subject of our last chapter, which is intended to throw some light on how the West relates to Eastern thought, in this context particularly to Vedanta. Because of the complexity of the subject it is obvious that only a few aspects can be discussed here. The religious and philosophical East-West dialogue cannot be covered in a chapter, nor indeed in a whole book. This will be a task for coming centuries—if we still have that much time left for it.

Vedanta and the West

THE VIEW IS OFTEN PUT FORWARD that Indian philosophy and the problems it deals with are so fundamentally different from Western thought that for the Westerner they can be little more than exotic subjects for study. If this were really so, it would remain incomprehensible why so many people in the West look particularly to Eastern religion and philosophy today for answers to questions concerning the deeper meaning of life. Clarification would moreover be needed to explain why so many thinkers who have exercised a decisive influence on Western philosophy—from Pythagoras to Plotinus and Eckhart and on to the leading philosophers of German Idealism—frequently advanced hypotheses that sound not a little "Vedantic." If comparisons must be made at all, much more differentiation is called for. Then we see that East and West are not two mutually exclusive entities; suddenly the position of an Indian philosopher is closer to that of a German thinker, such as Schelling, than to the world of his northeastern neighbor, a Chinese sage.

EASTERN MYSTICISM AND CHRISTIANITY

When Western Christian theology debates Eastern religious systems such as Vedanta these days, its criticism repeats much that has always been used in arguments in the West against Plotinus, John Scotus Erigena, Eckhart, or even Spinoza. This always involves the defense of a personal god (already being the absolute); the uniqueness of the human individual (as created by him); the seriousness of original sin and the necessity of salvation "from above." It is often possible to come up with Vedantic counterarguments by citing Plotinus or Spinoza; that is, by employing the language of a *philosophia perennis* which stubbornly survived alongside official church doctrine, even in the West, and, despite dissimilitude of time and place, has remained surprisingly unchanged. The almost indefinable "one" of Plotinus, the Nirguna Brahman of Vedanta, the shunyata (void) of Mahayana Buddhism, the supra-personal Tao, Eckhart's "source of the divinity"—it is as if the biblical creator-god were beleaguered by a unified front of negatives, by an "it" that does not "will" anything, but simply "is," or more precisely: neither is nor is not. When a "Creation" is accepted at all in these teachings, it is only as a kind of emanation from the one, as apparent separation from the absolute—never as involving a unique act of will.

We have already alluded to this distinct difference: that, according to Vedanta, something is not "there" because God created it out of nothing (and could just as well *not* have created it), but because the infinite, by virtue of its own maya, *appears* to have become finite—without, of course, really relinquishing its transcendency. Anyone overlooking this significant difference in any East-West dia-

logue will be talking right past the other side, because two
fundamentally different ways of explaining existence are
colliding here—in turn also affecting all other theological
and philosophical notions, particularly those concerning
salvation and release. A Christian usually looks on himself
as a sinner and knows himself reconciled to God by the
atonement of Christ's death on the cross—provided he
creates the conditions for it by fervently believing in redemption and leading a life worthy of it. The Vedantic ideal
of the jivanmukta, the "one enlightened in this body,"
must strike a Christian as blasphemy when he applies his
traditional anthropology here. But in the Vedantic
understanding—as also in the Platonic and neo-Platonic
understanding—what really matters is *re-membering* one's
original unity with the divine. After a sometimes enchant-
ing, sometimes terrifying journey through the finite maya-
worlds where it plays this or that role, the infinite finds its
way back to itself—to discover at the moment of enlightenment that it has actually never left, because it knows neither
time, nor space, nor causality, neither a before nor an after.
Our finite nature is always absorbed—in a sense "taken
care of"—in an eternal *now*. This is why the Vedantin
never quite understands why Christians attach such importance to events in time, such as the Fall from Grace, the act
of Redemption by Christ on the cross, and like points of
doctrine. How can events, occurring as they do in the realm
of maya, affect our true Self for better or for worse? The
Atman neither decreases nor increases, it only appears to us
to take on various forms and, while "exiled" in maya, to
"partake" of the finite. The Christian can think of a
"black" soul; in Vedanta, a "black" Atman is unthinkable.

The Christian theologian who not only struggles, hopes,
and fears by his faith, but in effect also thinks by it, must

rely on a metaphysics which frequently seems almost at cross-purposes with his Christian impulses. There have been many Western thinkers, of course, who philosophized in the simple belief that in Christianity the human mind reached its fullest potential; but on closer inspection one sees that many of them tended to philosophize in the belief that Christianity would find its fullest potential in their own particular system. So the Kierkegaards promptly appeared on the scene to rap the Hegels over the knuckles and prove to them that their grand systems had little to do with "real" Christianity.

Now, as justified as it may be to emphasize Christianity's existential dimension, doing so can lead to a sharp division between religion and philosophy. Someone who is in search of eternal principles—beyond a life determined by personal existential crises, beyond faith and hope (and fear and trembling!)—may find himself occasionally compelled to take leave from being an "existential" Christian and give himself over to the Platonic or Vedantic spirit, a spirit always concerned with ultimate questions. At least when it comes to being, to being rooted in the source, these traditions seem to offer a better form of help than traditional Christianity.

The religious East-West dialogue still being in its initial phase we cannot yet foresee what results it will eventually produce. A great deal of mistrust has to be overcome: mistrust of mysticism and of a supposed "pantheism," to mention only two examples. Characteristically, Christianity has an easier time today where it is faced with a path that is totally different from its own, such as is the case with Zen Buddhism, which does not involve a personal creator-god or a divine incarnation. Here one can focus just on meditation, on actual practice, without having to contend too much with theological questions. One does, of course, attempt to compare the impersonal nature of Zen with a religion of love for the personal god and one's fellow man, yet the total otherness of Zen also elicits bows of respect for this very otherness on the part of some Christians who are almost grateful for the clarity of this distinctly different approach. One tends to find it a welcome complement to the practice of prayer—without it encroaching on the actual content of the Christian faith.

Things look quite different when Christianity grapples with Hinduism and Vedanta. While here, too, it finds well-established meditation practices, it is at the same time up against no less well-established "theological" systems where the personal god, the concept of divine incarnation, grace, and similar ideas are by no means absent. Those who tried to avoid a genuine confrontation used to either refer to Vedanta (and often *all* of Hinduism) as one of those "rather vague Eastern wisdom religions" without knowledge of a personal god as such, or regard the theistic features in Indian religion as failed attempts to approximate the Christian truth—as exotic bowdlerizations, so to speak.

But what makes Vedanta so complex and fascinating—and also challenging—is that within it we find both pure Advaita and strong theistic tendencies: sometimes seen as different stages one above the other; sometimes as views opposed to each other; and sometimes as views existing alongside each other—with the theistic tendency winning out completely in popular Hinduism. We actually find *within* Vedanta itself some of the same tensions that attend Christianity's confrontations with other religions and philosophical systems that reject a personal god—or at least show no particular interest in his existence. A study of the various views within Vedanta would surely prove profitable for many Christian theologians. It might be even more fruitful, however, to also consider the possibility of an open universal system that looks on the personal and impersonal god as two aspects of one divine reality, as we find with Ramakrishna, for example.

This way of looking at things is, of course, not entirely foreign to Christianity; as we said before, one need only think of the Areopagites, of John Scotus Erigena, of Eckhart and other mystics. Here, as in the dialogue with the East, all depends on whether this direction can be considered as "orthodox" Christian—or only as an undercurrent which has not much to do with Christianity as such but belongs more to neo-Platonism. Any Christian who shares Eckhart's distinction between a supra-personal "Divinity" and the personal god will not have great difficulties with the "theology" of Advaita Vedanta. Before a serious dialogue with the Eastern religions can take place, therefore, clarification is needed within the Christian community itself as to what exactly is Christian and what is not.

There are two things the Western Christian could gain from a study of Vedanta. He could first of all take a closer look at certain contents of the maya-doctrine, particularly certain ways in which Vedanta tries to answer questions concerning the deeper meaning of relative existence. Among these are, for instance, the teaching of reincarnation (the idea that each individual soul must reembody until it has realized its true nature, its unity with the divine); the related Law of Karma (the principle that reward and punishment are automatic consequences, whether in life here on earth or in any other world); the concept of the avatar (the teaching that God periodically incarnates in human form); and the idea of Creation as a constant process of renewal, among others. Second, and more important, he can draw inspiration from the spirit of radical Advaita and—sweeping aside all these specific questions, however important they may be—he can try to formulate the answers based on the rational interpretation of revealed truth, when he will, of course, find them not to yield so easily to formulations. Someone who has never been consumed by a longing for the ultimate answer is not likely to penetrate to the heart of Vedanta or of mysticism as such.

Concerning the specific questions above, the Western Christian must also continue to reexamine his own views to see whether he does not, perhaps, occasionally confuse a cherished shell with its content. In the otherness of Vedanta he encounters new ways of looking at himself and the world which could quite possibly even beneficially affect his Christian view of the world. Deep and sincere study of another worldview sharpens the eye for what is essential in one's own teaching, as distinguished from merely historical and cultural accretions. We must all try to get beyond the din of the warring religious factions of the early centuries to reach a greater openness where the dialogue with the spiritual world of the East can be fully included. Of course, certain areas were sectioned off long ago; as when, for instance, a line of demarcation was drawn between Christianity and neo-Platonism. But it is precisely these questions which have a chance today to be seen in a new light through a dialogue with Buddhism and Vedanta—all the more so since it has been shown that such questions and problems have continued to stir in the dark and were often enough seeking the light of day in the writings of individual philosophers and mystics.

REFLECTIONS IN WESTERN PHILOSOPHY
AND LITERATURE

In European philosophy we come across points of contact with the Vedantic worldview at every turn. The pre-Socratic philosophers' quest for the ultimate *physis,* or nature of things, reminds one of the quest of the Upanishadic seers for "the One by knowing which all else is known." Here as there, almost imperceptibly, the material shades off into the immaterial; the penultimate—infinite space or energy—becomes a symbol for the ultimate, about which it is no longer possible to assert anything. The sharp distinction Parmenides made, between pure being and the world of appearances, reminds one of the later Vedantic distinctions between a pure Advaita and a changeable maya-world. Heraclitus' rather more dynamic worldview, his *panta-rhei* or eternal flux—the cyclic nature of the universe forever consuming and renewing itself in the great fire—and his conception of the soul as limitless, also have an Eastern ring. The harmony of the spheres of the great initiate Pythagoras, and Plato's famous parable of the cave, also make Greece seem even nearer to India than to Israel.

Particularly characteristic of thinkers whose ideas border on Vedanta is a certain unity of mysticism and philosophy. We see this in the case of great "jnanis" like Plotinus and Meister Eckhart, both of whom discoursed with great lucidity about their bold mystical speculations, yet at the same time with the ardor and enthusiasm almost worthy of a bhakta. They are the "sober drunkards" who, well acquainted with the "other" state, speak of the suprapersonal *one* with the same fervor as others do only when speaking of the "living God of Abraham, Isaac, and Jacob."

We still find a faint reflection of this in German Idealism, but it is indeed often only a faint afterglow. The absolute "I" of Fichte, for example, despite its strong spiritual undercurrent, all too often resembles more a Prussian caricature of the Indian Atman. With Hegel—who in his youth still spread the Gospel of the Kingdom of God, together with Hölderlin and other like-minded young men— philosophy soon cut loose from its nourishing foundation in mysticism: his absolute *Zeitgeist* (spirit of the times) was at best only a gleam in the eye of Napoleon as he marched into Jena, not the brightness in the eye of one enlightened, one who has realized the Brahman "beyond history and lacking nothing." Schelling remained, perhaps, closest to the spirit of mysticism, but his attempt, especially in his later work, to make Christianity the foundation of his philosophy, proved that the Christian spirit is not very compatible with philosophizing. Schelling thus became a tragic phenomenon; his contemporaries could look on in fascination as a once youthfully bold, almost Vedantic-seeming "I" or Self, equating itself with the absolute, gradually took on the features of an aging sage contemplating Gnostic profundities and trying to bring Alexandrian and Boehmenian thinking into accord with Christian orthodoxy—all the while stumbling increasingly over "the given," the undeniable forces of nature and history. Something about this is reminiscent of Aurobindo, especially the distance he put between himself and an all-too-loudly proclaimed I-monism, and his increasing leanings toward the craggy world of prakriti. But the difference between the two men—Aurobindo, the practicing yogi, and Schelling, the "philosopher"—is also particularly evident here.

Kant's quest for the *thing-in-itself* remained limited to the purely philosophical approach. Not unlike the Vedantin, he saw the mesh of space, time, and causality as precisely what gets between us and the true nature of things, that is, as *the* obstacle. Here this great thinker reached the limits of thought, and we have to be grateful to him for being honest about it. Yet his example also demonstrates that Western philosophy was no longer rooted in, and supported by, a meditative tradition that could have helped this great philosopher pierce the veil of maya in mystic insight. In Kant's system religion is really reduced to mere ethics. Particularly his most brilliant examples demonstrate the progressive impoverishment and drying-up of the spiritual-intellectual culture of the West.

Even Schopenhauer is no exception to this. His enthusiasm for the Upanishads did not diminish the egocentricity and sullenness of his nature. He, too, altogether lacked the humus-rich soil of tradition from which he could have drawn the real sap of life. Known as a man whose main profession was "thinking" (and for the regularity of his daily walks at the accustomed hour) this German philosopher may in many of his thoughts have actually touched on the world of the Vedantic rishis and the Buddha; but he himself was unable to get beyond these "thoughts." For the Eastern sage it is only beyond thought where true realization begins.

Nietzsche finally proves that the West had reached a critical impasse. He, too, now and then stole a glance at the East, especially in connection with taking a swipe at Christianity; but his mental affliction had progressed to a point where his almost excruciating clear-sightedness, rather than leading to transcendence of ordinary consciousness, led to insanity instead. What in the Indian tradition is brought about slowly and organically with the help of a guru—the gradual growth into the divine dimension, man's true home—was here struggling for realization in fits and spasms. A negative Western Christian anthropology was striking back here: in a kind of overreaction, Nietzsche cursed all Christian morality and could not bear the thought that, should a god exist at all, he should not be a god himself. While rejecting a moralizing god he wished for a dancing god. Something was trying to shake free here, something long ago come free in the East; indeed, something oftentimes part of orthodox teaching there. Nietzsche would probably have found his god in Shiva. During his twilight years, the very years of his increasing insanity, Vivekananda was calling out to his Western audiences: "You are all gods!"

These sketches are, of course, done in rather broad strokes, but we do not want to fall into the error of painting things just in black and white. Contemplated individually and in greater detail, we can be endlessly inspired by the writings of the thinkers we touched on so briefly here; and many more names could be added. Nevertheless, the impression that Western philosophy at some time or other lost the "golden thread," its larger context, can perhaps not altogether be dismissed out of hand. The ladders of thought rise boldly upward—then end in empty space. Certain more recent attempts to find the broken end of the thread again, such as those of Heidegger for instance, are certainly most deserving of recognition; yet what we are left with in the end is only a murmuring congregation gathering somewhat irresolutely in the house of being. Compared with the rugged originality of the hitherto unbroken native Indian tradition, the language of today's philosopher concerned with being often sounds a little contrived. Philosophy in the West tends to be more authentic and robust when, as is the case with Bloch, it spreads a gospel of hope through active humanitarian commitment. If the East is to be enriched by the West it is more likely going to come from this direction.

When looking for points of contact with the mood and spirit of Vedanta in Western literature, a sense of the maya-like nature of the world is surely the most noteworthy feature. Western man also has often looked on the world as a stage, a dream, something fleeting and questionable; one has only to think of Shakespeare and many dramas of the baroque. Later Romantics proclaimed, on the one hand, a nearly pantheistic sense of the oneness of things, but on the other also suffered under what they perceived as an almost unbearable tension between the finite and the infinite. This tension was in part lessened by the introduction of the famous *Romantic Irony,* but in part also further exacerbated by it. Romanticism was, after all, Platonism revived, and it shared with the latter the sorrows engendered by viewing the world of appearances as unreal. One need only read the following lines by Jean Paul to realize how close even a Western poet can come to an awareness that all is merely maya. In his *Hesperus,* he writes: "And when on the way he looked up at the blackish-blue sky, where wandering clouds were strewn about the moon like cinders, and then quickly back over the half-hidden shadowy surroundings, over the shadowy hills and shadowy villages, everything seemed to him to be dead, empty, and vain; and it seemed to him as if in some brighter world there was a magic-lantern, and through the lantern passed glass slides with earths and springs and clusters of people painted on them—and we called the flickering shadowy pictures coming from these slides 'us' and 'earth' and 'life'—and all this colorful display was being pursued by a great big shadow."[31] Or in *The Invisible Box:* "I sat down on the steps of an altar, around me the moonlight with the dusky, rushing shadows of the clouds; my soul was aloft; I addressed the 'I,' which I still was: 'Who are you? Who is sitting here and remembers and is in pain? You, I, something . . . where did the painted clouds go which for thirty years travelled past this "I," and which I called childhood, youth and life?'—My self passed through this colored mist—but I could not grasp it—from a distance it seemed something solid, on myself only dewdrops trickling away—or what we call moments—so life is this trickling from one moment into the next, this dewdrop of time. . . ."[32]

Again and again we come upon this sensation of unreality in modern literature. "The feeling of having solid ground under my feet and a firm skin about me, so natural to most people, is not very strongly developed in me,"[33] we read in Robert Musil's novel *The Man without Qualities;* and it is surely no coincidence that Ulrich, the antihero of the book, and his sister Agathe seek refuge in "another" state. The mysticism of a Meister Eckhart and of Vedanta is never far away here. But it is also no coincidence that all these attempts are ultimately doomed to fail; because they are no longer sustained by a living tradition, they take place in a vacuum.

Another writer who often came very close to the spirit of mysticism was Franz Kafka. He once wrote that man cannot live without an enduring trust in something indestructible within himself, even though what it is may forever remain hidden from him. There are many passages in the writings of this highly perceptive author which clearly reflect the maya-nature of the world.

"Seen with the tainted earthly eye," he once noted, "we

find ourselves in the situation of rail passengers in the midst of an accident in a long tunnel, and this at a point where the light at the beginning of the tunnel can no longer be seen, while the light at the end of the tunnel is so small that the eye constantly seeks and loses it, such that beginning and end are not even certain. But in the confusion of the senses, or their overwroughtness, we have all kinds of monsters all around us and, depending on the mood and injury of each, the kaleidoscopic patterns either excite or exhaust us."[34]

EUROPE AND AMERICA

When we examine more closely how Vedantic ideas—and Eastern ideas in general—were taken up in the West, we notice that reactions in Europe and America were not the same. It seems that in Europe, around the turn of the century, those who took an interest in Eastern spiritual culture were for the most part people already given to much solemn reflection. The dominant trait was often a rather pessimistic view of the world; someone like Alfred Kubin, the Austrian artist, for instance, spoke of "Buddhistic crises." The spirit of Schopenhauer was still in evidence everywhere, and this mixture of a German sense of the profundity of things and a certain somberness exists to this day in some circles. Hermann Hesse represents a somewhat freer version of this encounter with the East, and it is hardly a coincidence that his books eventually became particularly popular in America.

Although America also had a philosophical tradition which was receptive to the wisdom of the East—we need only think of Emerson—assimilation was in other respects a great deal more informal there. It may well have been that the dynamic spirit of Vivekananda had something to do with this—but by the end of the last century, at any rate, Vedanta had become much affected there by the pioneering optimism, the easygoing democratic openness, and a cult of youth and health; unfortunately, however, also often by a boundless naiveté and a certain shallowness. One need only read the essays of Prentice Mulford to get a feeling for this mixture of insightfulness and a typical American philosophy of success. Mulford died two years before the arrival of Vivekananda in America; yet much of what can be found in the way of "positive thinking" in Mulford's essays can—in Vedantic language—also be found in the talks of the Indian swami. Vivekananda himself seems to have had little objection to his Advaita falling on the fertile ground of American democracy. But he was also not unaware of the negative side of the spiritual scene in America: the false expectations and the risk of commercialization to which yoga had already fallen prey. In one of his last talks, "Is Vedanta the Religion of the Future" (1900), Vivekananda expressed great skepticism concerning the possibility of true Vedanta having a widespread effect. He was anything but elitist, but he also knew that, generally, people promptly suffuse spiritual ideas with their own egoistic and materialistic motives.

The difficult situation Vivekananda encountered in the West at that time has not become better today; on the contrary it has, if anything, become even more confusing. But it also produced positive phenomena then. In Europe, for instance, there were writers like Romain Rolland—acquainting his readers with the thought-world of Ramakrishna and Vivekananda—and scientists like the physicist Erwin Schrödinger who saw, particularly in Vedanta, the possibility for a synthesis between science and metaphysics. In America, too, many writers were coming in contact with the Vedanta movement, among them J. D. Salinger, Henry Miller, and especially Aldous Huxley and Christopher Isherwood. For some this contact remained a brief episode; for others, like Isherwood, it became a turning point in their lives. Most of those interested in Vedanta came from elevated intellectual circles which rejected the dogmatism of the Christian churches yet longed for spirituality and satisfactory answers to the fundamental questions of existence. In Vedanta they found a wide-open, universal, and philosophically oriented religion where even the penetrating scientific mind could find something to its taste. The spiritual orientation of the swamis of the Ramakrishna Mission ensured that things went beyond mere intellectual debate, that is, that philosophical insight was also accompanied by meditative practice.

Soon wave after wave of spiritual import from India followed. In the course of this, Europeans were often at a disadvantage because some of these Indian spiritual traditions reached them only by way of North America. Names like Ramakrishna, Vivekananda, and even Vedanta repeatedly came up during the postwar period, but these names were not the ones making the headlines. The reasons for this are both positive and negative. On the positive side it should be stressed that the groups associated with traditional Vedanta tend to prefer quiet work and, therefore, have little interest in making headlines. Negatively viewed, however, many a group seems to lack the flexibility necessary to adjust to new impulses, most of which are coming from young people. Instead of creatively building on the enormous spiritual impetus given by figures like Ramakrishna and Vivekananda, they frequently content themselves with merely "administering" their spiritual heritage, just as they tend to hold on to Shankara's "eternal truths" and to classical Advaita Vedanta as such. This quiet activity behind the scenes may be a relief to some—especially when contrasted with the commercial clamor surrounding many a sectarian group—but an important element and necessary complement to tranquillity and close study of the texts that is all too often missing is *vitality*. Those who are content with being the preservers and keepers of the Upanishads will never actualize their true spirit and be able to pass it on to others—a spirit which was, after all, originally one of new departures. A Vedanta which does not fully expose itself to the present is not much more than a fossil: of interest at best to academics.

A LIVING SYNTHESIS

One reason for Vedanta's lack of vitality and flexibility may be that Shakti, the active, creative principle—forever making things "new" again—has for too long been misconstrued and undervalued. Here the great Vedanta system reveals its weakness, that is, as a *system*. Here we probably also find the explanation for the curious lack of productivity of Indian philosophy in modern times. If we earlier reproached Western philosophers with having lost the thread connecting them with an older tradition, we must in turn now reproach Indian philosophers with often having attached too much importance to tradition and with endlessly chewing over old material as if this was all philosophy was about. (We are, of course, mainly referring to the academic scene, the universities and such, not to innovators like Vivekananda or Aurobindo.) One sometimes longs for more creativity—even at the risk of error. It may well be that this longing is related to our Christian heritage, a heritage which, it is true, has also often run the risk of being content with what seems well rounded and whole, with so-called "eternal truths," but which has also again and again flown the banners of challenge and hope.

Today the necessity for coming to terms with the spirit of the times should be particularly obvious to Vedantins where typically inappropriate attitudes are concerned. Anyone not carefully analyzing such situations must soon experience his philosophy and religion being used as alibis to persist in living undisturbed with aberrant attitudes—much of which can be covered up with the ideological cloak of Vedantic and Buddhist wisdom. The reluctance of many people today to enter into genuine commitments is then suddenly declared to be in tune with Buddhist or Hindu egolessness. With the requisite cynicism the excesses of our throwaway society can then be rationalized as "Vedantic non-attachment." After all, the scriptures of Eastern mysticism speak of the necessity not to be "attached" to either people or things, do they not? What is often overlooked is that in Eastern cultures reverence and respect have always been taken for granted quite naturally and have, therefore, usually not required particular exhortation. In our cultures, however, such preconditions can often no longer be assumed. Without respect and a great deal of love for one's fellow human, the Atman doctrine—because of its relatively impersonal character—brings with it obvious dangers. The Atman teaching is at the core of Vedanta, and it also could easily fill a sensitive gap in Christianity. Yet

Christianity—and Humanism—may rightfully also point out Vedanta's weakness, which is that between the almost impersonal Atman and the also quite impersonal gunas (Nature's dispositions) and *koshas* (sheaths), the living individual is often forgotten.

The ever-progressing depersonalization of the modern world, especially in the big cities, requires the Vedantin to give more thought to the value of the individual and the I/thou dimension (so insistently pleaded for by Martin Buber); for he can hardly claim that this depersonalization and ever-increasing anonymity are nothing more than mankind's progress toward the ultimate Vedantic insight, that the ego is an illusion. The ego may indeed lastly be an illusion. But when we see these ultimate truths so terribly misappropriated, it is perhaps time to reformulate them so as to preclude mistaken notions. What should above all be looked into is whether the Atman does not also have its positive reflection in the finite, relative world—for example, as heightened alertness, love, creativity, indeed as individual uniqueness. For if we take Advaita at its word, we are not only all made equal by the Atman teaching, but each individual already *is* the absolute. And whenever referring back to true Advaita and the Upanishads *alone* fails to help us on, why not fill some of the gaps with Christian ethics? It would surely not hurt the Atman to do this.

All this clearly shows that when Vedanta—like any other religion and ideology—addresses the world today, it cannot do so isolated from what is going on around it, that it must analyze the present situation before deciding on its priorities. (Is it really necessary, for instance, to extol as wisdom's ultimate end the detached and merely witnessing consciousness of the Vedantin to someone who regularly spends his evenings staring at television, someone who lives life practically secondhand? Would it not be better to inspire him to get up out of his armchair and do something creative, that is, to try to mobilize whatever remains in him of real feelings?)

The question today is no longer whether one of the great world religions and ideologies is better than the other. What matters is that they complement each other. This does, of course, require a certain degree of humility, a willingness to learn, and an admission of the limitations of one's own "system." Every religion has its strengths and weaknesses. The strength of Vedanta lies, doubtless, in its metaphysical breadth; against this background Christian theology sometimes seems quite petty and narrow. The strength of Christianity, on the other hand, lies in its ethics, in the impetus it gives to loving one's fellow human, in active, committed engagement. It can do Vedanta no harm to be inspired a little by these impulses—indeed even be infected by this "sting" of neighborly love—if it does not want to suffocate in its own symmetry and metaphysical greatness. Just as one cannot forever feed on hope, one cannot forever derive nourishment from a spiritual superstructure.

Vivekananda must have felt this when he wrote to an Indian Muslim friend: ". . . I am firmly persuaded that without the help of practical Islam, theories of Vedantism, however fine and wonderful they may be, are entirely valueless to the vast mass of mankind. . . . Vedanta brain and Islam body, that is the only hope."[35] Vivekananda was, of course, thinking above all of India; hence the stress on Islam. Applied to the world as a whole one could just as well replace "Islam" here with "Christianity." Vivekananda was not concerned with this or that particular religion, but he did feel that the lofty metaphysics of Vedanta needed something to supplement it, some form of "embodiment." Hinduism, with all its caste restrictions and other limitations, did not seem to him the most suitable form for incarnating Advaita among human society as a whole. Although he often spoke of a "practical Vedanta," daily experience must have taught him that Christians and Muslims achieved more in this respect than most Vedantins.

Vivekananda's proposed solution—Vedantic head, Islamic (Christian) body—was, of course, not entirely without problems either. At least such a division was not to lead to a situation where Vedantins would regard themselves as a purely metaphysically oriented elite—that is, as the smart "head" of the movement—while implementation, or, to put it more bluntly, the social dirty-work, would be left to Muslims and Christians. This would only make for a new caste system. Vivekananda simply based his idea on the evidence that sages of the Vedantic tradition had concerned themselves hitherto with the highest metaphysical cosmology but had somewhat neglected this earth, while Muslims and Christians—despite all the theology and philosophy which they, too, possessed—had always been concerned, too, with brotherly equality and the improvement of this world. The time seemed to have come for both attitudes to come together, the universality of Vedanta (often given too much to dwelling on generalities) and the ethic thrust of the Semitic religions (which, while devoted to concrete everyday work among the people, also unfortunately often combined this active commitment with fanaticism and narrow-mindedness).

It is not always easy to build bridges between Eastern metaphysics and mysticism, on the one hand, and, on the other, Western Christian ethics. Albert Schweitzer considered these two worlds ultimately irreconcilable, however much he admired the one and lived in the other. But can we live forever in a world thus divided? True Advaita will probably become fully incarnate here on earth only when the impulse of Christian neighborly love and the infinite breadth of Vedantic mysticism have joined to transform the face of this earth.

RUTH L. ROCKWOOD MEMORIAL LIBRARY
THE PUBLIC LIBRARY OF LIVINGSTON
Robert H. Harp Dr.
Livingston, N. J. 07039

Notes

For selections from the Upanishads and the Bhagavad Gita, the translations of Swami Nikhilananda have been used by permission of the Ramakrishna-Vivekananda Center, New York. Excerpts from the Vivekacudamani and the Ashtavakra Samhita are based on Swami Madhavananda's translations (Almora, Himalayas, 1932); brief passages from German literature were rendered into English specifically for this volume.

1. Abhishiktananda, *The Farther Shore* (Delhi, 1975), 63.
2. Swami Vivekananda, *Complete Works* (Calcutta: Advaita Ashram, 1964), vol. V, 235.
3. R.T.H. Griffith, trans., *Rgveda, Samaveda, White Yahurveda, Atharvaveda* (Benares, 1895–1907).
4. A. A. MacDonnell, trans., *Hymn from the Rigveda* (London, 1922).
5. *Sacred Books of the East,* vol. XV, 27.
6. Robert Musil, *Der Mann ohne Eigenschaften* [The Man without Qualities] (Hamburg-Reinbek: Rowohlt Verlag), 252.
7. Ibid., 119.
8. Betty Heimann, *Die Tiefschlafspekulation der alten Upanishaden* [The Deep-Sleep Speculation of the Old Upanishads] (Munich-Neubiberg, 1922).

9. Heinrich Zimmer, *Der Weg zum Selbst, Lehre und Leben des Shri Ramana Maharshi* [The Path to the Self: Teachings and Life of Ramana Maharshi] (Cologne: Eugen-Diederichs Verlag, 1976), 90–92.

10. Bernard R. Blackney, trans., *Meister Eckhart* (New York: Harper & Bros., 1941), Introduction.

11. Ibid., 231.

12. St. Thomas Aquinas, *Quaestiones disputae de Malo,* I.3.

13. ———, *Quaestiones disputatae de potentia Dei,* III.16.

14. ———, *Summa contra gentiles,* 3.I.12.

15. Swami Nikhilananda, trans., *The Gospel of Shri Ramakrishna by "M"* (New York: Ramakrishna-Vivekananda Center, 1942), 867.

16. *Worte des Ramakrishna* [Words of Ramakrishna] (Zurich: Rotapfel-Verlag, 1930), 145.

17. Ibid., 142–143.

18. Ibid., 363.

19. Swami Nikhilananda, *The Gospel of Shri Ramakrishna,* 133–135 *passim.*

20. Ibid.

21. Ibid., 682.

22. Ibid., 135–139 *passim.*

23. Swami Vivekananda, *Works,* vol. III, 340.

24. Ibid., 128–129.

25. Ibid., 151–152.

26. Ibid., 291.

27. Ibid., 87.

28. *Shri Aurobindo on Himself and on the Mother* (Pondicherry, 1953), 204–205.

29. Ibid., 776.

30. Swami Vivekananda, *Works,* vol. V, 31.

31. *Jean Paul: Werk, Leben, Wirkung* [Jean Paul: Work, Life, Influence] (Munich: Piper Verlag, 1963), 96.

32. Ibid., 50.

33. Musil, *Der Mann ohne Eigenschaften*, 289.

34. Franz Kafka, *Hochzeitsvorbereitungen auf dem Lande und andere Prosa aus dem Nachlass* [Wedding Preparations in the Country and Other Prose from the Estate] (Frankfurt: S. Fischer-Verlag, 1953), 73.

35. Swami Vivekananda, *Works*, vol. VI, 416.

Glossary

acharya   Religious teacher; founder of a religio-philosophical school.

Advaita   Literally "not-two," non-duality; school of Vedanta according to which there is only one reality—the Brahman—and all multiplicity merely illusion (maya).

Advaitin   Follower of the Advaita teaching.

ahamkara   Literally "I-maker"; the mental "organ" responsible for "I-consciousness."

ahimsa   The virtue of non-injury.

ananda   Divine joy, highest bliss.

anna   Food; substance of the gross physical body.

arhat   Early Buddhist ascetic.

Arjuna   Hero of the Mahabharata epic and one of the Pandava brothers to whom, at the beginning of the battle of Kurukshetra, Krishna reveals the wisdom teaching contained in the Bhagavad Gita.

asura   Demon.

Atman   The indestructible real Self behind the superficial personality.

avatar   Literally "descent"; a divine incarnation.

225

avidya   Nescience, blindness.

Bhagavad Gita   Lit. "Song of the Lord"; a short book in verse (composed 100 B.C.–A.D. 100) embodying the principles of the religious life as espoused by the later Hinduism. See also Mahabharata.

Bhagavan   An epithet of the personal god as Lord of Creation; also a term of respect for a holy man.

bhakta   Someone who worships the personal god and follows the Path of Loving Devotion.

bhakti   Loving devotion; worship of the personal god (in whatever manifestation).

Bheda-Abheda   School of Vedanta according to which the Brahman and Creation are both separate and not separate.

Brahmā   Creator-demiurge; the first figure in the Hindu trimurti (Brahmā, Vishnu, and Shiva).

Brahma Sutras   (Also Vedanta Sutras): a Vedanta treatise in which an attempt was made to combine into one system the inspired wisdom of the Upanishads in the form of brief aphorisms.

buddhi   Enlightened intellect, higher intuition.

Chaitanya   Bengali saint who lived around A.D. 1500 and whom a Vedantic bhakti school claims as its authority.

chit   Knowledge, consciousness.

darshanas   Lit., "ways of seeing" or "points of view"; the six orthodox systems of Hinduism.

dharana   Concentration.

dharma   Duty, virtue; the correct way; religion practiced.

dhyana   Meditation.

Durga   One of the names of the Mother Goddess.

Dvaita   Lit., "two"; dualistic school of Vedanta.

Gaudapada   Radical exponent of the Advaita doctrine and forerunner of Shankara.

Gita   Short for Bhagavad Gita.

guna   Lit., "thread," "strand." The gunas are natural qualities of prakriti (primordial Nature or matter). See also tamas, rajas, and sattva.

guru   Spiritual teacher.

Hari   An epithet of Vishnu.

hatha-yoga   The yoga path devoted mainly to physical practice.

Hiranyagarbha   Lit., "Golden Germ" (also Seed, Egg); the personal creator-god Brahmā.

Indra   Vedic deity.

Ishvara   The personal god as Creator, Preserver, and Destroyer.

jiva   The individual embodied soul still tied to the round of birth-and-death.

jivanmukta   One enlightened who while still in this life has freed himself from the bonds of maya.

jnana   Knowledge; both highest knowledge itself and the process of gaining perfect insight.

jnana-yoga   The Path of Knowledge.

jnana-kanda   The part of the Vedic books devoted to knowledge of the highest truth.

jnani   Someone on the Path of Knowledge; in its ideal sense, one who is enlightened and realizes his oneness with the Brahman.

Kali   One of the names of the Mother Goddess.

karma   Deed, action, "works," and the good and bad consequences resulting from them.

karma-kanda   The part of the Vedas dealing with ritual worship.

karma-yoga   The yoga of action, or "works," originally relating particularly to the world of ritual and sacrifice; later the Path of Selfless Action in general.

kosha   The "sheaths" enveloping the Atman, from the gross physical body to the intellect.

Krishna   Incarnation of Vishnu who in the Bhagavad Gita discloses himself as the highest Lord of Creation (Purushottama).

Kshatriya   Warrior caste (which also supplied kings and officials).

Mahabharata   Great Epic. Mainly an account of the war between the Kauravas and the Pandavas; the Bhagavad Gita is only one episode in this voluminous epic.

Mahamaya   The Mother Goddess as the great "magician" and embodiment of maya, which she herself transcends.

mahat First manifestation from the womb of primordial Nature (prakriti): cosmic intelligence.

Mahavakya Great Words; key pronouncements summarizing the highest Vedantic knowledge.

manas The mind, also disposition and volition.

maya Illusion, mirage, trick; the "appearance" of the absolute: positively, God's creative power; negatively, the veil of diversity hiding the *one*.

Mayaveda The school of Vedanta founded by Shankara central to which is the maya doctrine.

neti, neti Lit., "Not this, not that"; the negative approach in Vedantic mysticism, its end being the attributeless, "naked" *one*.

Nirguna Brahman Lit., "Brahman without gunas," that is, without qualifying characteristics or attributes; the Brahman not subject to any assertions.

nirvikalpa samadhi The state of unself-conscious absorption in which all duality ceases to exist.

OM Archaic mystic syllable (also AUM); the divine "Word" whence everything proceeds.

paramatman The Atman in its transcendent aspect, in contrast to the embodied individual soul.

Patanjali Formulator of the classical yoga system and author of the celebrated Yoga Sutras.

prakriti Primordial matter (or Nature) from which all of Creation exfoliates.

pralaya "Cosmic sleep" of Creation at cyclical intervals.

prana Breath, breathing; the life-force, energy.

Puranas Ancient lore: myths and legends.

purusha Lit., "Primal Man"; person, man. In the Sankhya system, the cosmic spirit or conscious principle which remains essentially unaffected by the entanglements of primordial Nature or matter (prakriti).

Purushottama The cosmic purusha. The term Krishna uses in the Bhagavad Gita when he refers to himself as the highest purusha, the one transcending both primordial Nature and the purusha's static, purely "onlooking" consciousness.

rajas The second of the three gunas: physical and mental activity, particularly of the ego-bound kind.

raja-yoga The "royal" yoga, identical with the classical yoga of Patanjali; the Path of Concentration and Meditation.

Ramanuja Founder of a theistic school of Vedanta.

rishi Seer, sage.

Rudra An epithet of Shiva.

Saguna Brahman Brahman with attributes; the personal god.

sahaja samadhi A state of naturally occurring awareness and absorption.

samadhi State of deep absorption; rapture.

samsara The round of birth and death; the relative world.

sanatana dharma Lit., "eternal religion"; the expression Hindus themselves use when referring to their religion.

Sankhya One of the six orthodox systems of Hinduism which makes a sharp distinction between a static consciousness (purusha) and an "active" Nature (prakriti).

sannyasin Monk who has renounced the worldly life.

sat Being.

Sat-chit-ananda (Also "Satchidananda"): Lit., "Being-Consciousness-Bliss," the Brahman expressed in positive terms.

sattva The highest of the gunas: intrinsic nature shining forth as the clear light of wisdom, beauty, and harmony.

satya Truth.

Shaivism Form of Hinduism in which Shiva is worshiped as the highest God.

Shakti The dynamic, creative power of the absolute conceived of as female; the Mother Goddess or Divine Mother.

Shankara Important Vedanta philosopher (about A.D. 800) who expanded the Advaita teaching into a comprehensive system.

shruti Lit., what was *heard;* revealed scripture: the Vedas and certain Upanishads.

shunyata Emptiness, void.

smriti Lit., what was *remembered;* the teachings of the ancient saints and sages and the books on law and ritual, i.e., (human) tradition.

tamas   The lowest of the three gunas: dullness, darkness, inertia.

tapas   Fervent asceticism; heat.

"Tat tvam asi"   Lit., "That thou art"; celebrated formula summarizing the Vedantic mysticism of identity.

trimurti   The "trilogy" of the Hindu personal god as Brahma, Vishnu, and Shiva.

turiya   Lit., "fourth"; the absolute state beyond waking, dreaming and dreamless sleep.

Upanishads   Collective name for the 108 books representing various philosophical interpretations of the Vedas, particularly the later ones (900–500 B.C.).

Vaishnavism   (Also Vashnuism): a form of Hinduism in which Vishnu (and his incarnations Rama and Krishna) is worshiped as the highest God.

Vedas   Earliest known hymns, ritual texts, and philosophical treatises of India (1500–500 B.C.).

vidya   Knowledge, realization.

Vishisht Advaita   Modified non-dualism; the Vedanta school of Ramanuja.

viveka   The ability to distinguish between what is eternal and what is transitory.

512152